Faith

Tim Costello

Faith

hardie grant books
MELBOURNE · LONDON

Published in 2016 by Hardie Grant Books

Hardie Grant Books (Australia)
Ground Floor, Building 1
658 Church Street
Richmond, Victoria 3121
www.hardiegrant.com.au

Hardie Grant Books (UK)
5th & 6th Floor
52–54 Southwark Street
London SE1 1UN
www.hardiegrant.co.uk

Cataloguing-in-Publication data is available from the National
Library of Australia.

Faith
ISBN 978 1 74379 192 9

Cover illustration by Marc Martin
Typesetting by Kirby Jones

Colour reproduction by Splitting Image Colour Studio
Printed in China by 1010 Printing International Limited

To Merridie, who has kept faith with me.

To Dr Thorwald Lorenzen, who has helped me understand and apply my faith to the times in which we live.

To the World Vision worldwide community, with whom I have shared faith in action for the last thirteen years.

Contents

Foreword

Encounters with Tim Costello are always memorable. Tim's voice commands your attention, in volume and meaning. He cries out to us, gets our attention and speaks to our common humanity — causing us to pause and consider the world from the perspective of those living on the margins.

Tim brings the plight of the most vulnerable into our homes, our churches, into country towns and into the halls of power and we are convinced to lend a hand, to engage and share our resources.

He invites us into a conversation where we discover a world in need of restoration and we are inspired to act.

His Christian faith is a lived experience. It is his lifeblood, which he describes as having 'nourished the foundations' of his life, making him who he is. As you will discover, his is a deep, broad, inclusive faith that loves and includes first, bringing people from across the spectrum of society together. This is what makes *Faith* an important message of hope and reconciliation in this time. While not all will agree with Tim's perspectives, this book is an invitation into a timely discussion, one that you can be assured he is up for!

Faith is also a window into the breadth of Tim's work and relationships with people from all corners of the earth. It shows what has shaped, challenged, inspired and disappointed him, as well as his frustrations with politics and social policy here in Australia and beyond.

He is well known for his public profile as a social justice advocate, a leader in civil life and a church representative. He has worked at the coal face of ministry in Melbourne, local politics in St Kilda and with World Vision Australia.

World Vision has been greatly blessed by Tim's fine leadership, which has led to millions of Australians being inspired to act to end poverty and bring relief to the world's most vulnerable. Tim plays an important leadership role in the sector here in Australia and on the international stage. I want to personally thank Tim for his continued service to the organisation and his unrelenting commitment to see the lives of the most vulnerable transformed.

This is Tim's faith story. He does not pretend to speak for the World Vision partnership, which has 45,000 staff internationally, drawn from so many Christian faith traditions and other faiths.

Enjoy your encounter with Tim. It's sure to inspire you to reflect on your values and how you live them out.

Donna Shepherd
Managing director of Creating Communities,
Director of World Vision International, World Vision Australia
and World Vision New Zealand

Introduction

I often feel fed up with faith. So much said in the name of God represents a God I do not believe in or want to have anything to do with. The public religious discourse is narrow, bigoted and judgemental. I cringe when I hear these attitudes from my Christian colleagues who believe they are speaking for God. Often I wonder how much these purported followers of Jesus actually know about him.

I could renounce my faith or try to start a new variant, but that seems unrealistic. I am stuck. Stuck because the truth is that my faith is my lifeblood. It has nourished the very foundations of my life and made me who I am. I have written before on hope; this is my attempt to do justice to faith.

I see that this is true in so many others who are part of this faith, the largest worldwide religious community. Like me, they have been touched, changed and given purpose by their faith. So, though fed up with it, I realise that without the Christian faith and its spirituality of connection to others I cannot live meaningfully. I have Buddhist, Muslim and Hindu friends who share this feeling about their respective faiths. They too feel caught: needing the beauty and meaning of their faith in order to be their best selves but also wanting to shed the violence done in its name. I cannot speak for them, but what follows is my spirituality, which has emerged from my faith story. Carl Jung said the lack of meaning in life is a soul sickness, the full extent and import of which we have not yet begun to comprehend. I wonder what Jung would say about our age if he were alive today. I suspect he might diagnose even more soul sickness. Most of us are much more affluent than the people of Jung's time, but now we see mass epidemics of depression and anxiety disorders, high suicide rates, family breakdown and addiction. Why, when we are affluent, are we not flourishing?

I think soul sickness is the right term to describe what we are facing. Maximising wealth can never change the nature of the beast: we are animals who need meaning and purpose. Equally, maximising happiness as the goal of life is not working for most. To approach life with the question 'What can I get?' rather than 'What can I give?' is to mistake happiness for purpose. This is a chronic mistake that results in many unhappy individuals. Happiness is not the goal, but rather a by-product of a deeper sense of purpose.

We all need something more than just the material in order to find meaning. Spirituality is the exploration of that hunger. At its essence spirituality is about a relationship and connection to something bigger — something transcendent. It inevitably involves faith. For me, without a spiritual connection to God I struggle to find a deeper connection to who I am, to my neighbour, to the stranger, and to the world around me.

To speak of spirituality can seem irrational when the norm is the secular. We mean at least three things when we speak of the secular: firstly, the falling away of religious practice and belief. Secondly, the emptying out of religion and faith from public spaces. Thirdly, the move from a situation where everyone believed in God or some higher being to one in which belief in God is understood to be one option among others (and is now the least plausible); it is no longer the default setting. This is a profound change in our democratic society, but I think we still have beliefs and even a spirituality that is hardly secular and yet shapes our behaviour, policies and votes.

I resent both religious fundamentalists and secular fundamentalists. Both come to the table with their minds made up. Both are willing to exclude the other from the conversation if they do not surrender their position. As Rumi said, 'Out beyond ideas of wrongdoing and right-doing there is a field. I will meet you out there.' My faith says God is inviting us to that field, no matter how sure we are that we know the truth. It takes a certain faith to walk out to that field.

In my study there's a whimsical picture of me at eighteen. I look into those eyes and wonder at how my faith has changed. I see someone then who was more focused on the internal than the external; someone who wanted not only to *do* good, but to *be* good. There was a clarity that I had to surrender to something outside myself to gain strength within myself.

I have tried to keep a journal as part of my spiritual disciplines since I was seventeen. When I look at my entries for November 1975 I am shocked to discover that for the day after Prime Minister of Australia Gough Whitlam's dismissal — a momentous national political event — there is nothing recorded about it. My focus was on an inner struggle around my envy of someone else and diarising my failure. And I come from a family interested in politics!

It has made me think of faith with the analogy of the growth of a large tree. Inside the trunk are rings, which tell of the tree's growth over many years. Each ring attests to a stage along the way. As I started to live more externally the next rings were about wanting to conquer the world and to focus on how things worked. I wanted to know how to develop my professional skills and gain worldly success rather than focus on why the world existed or my character and calling. All this took place in a culture that encourages self-promotion and material success. I later realised that the next rings I added to my tree of faith were less about internal criteria and integrity and that I had strayed from a deeper inner purpose to self-purpose and pride. But these rings are still part of the same tree. I still have a strong faith and my accumulation of years has not obliterated the God experience.

I have always been suspicious of a formula called 'the stages of faith' that suggests a religious progress upwards beyond fundamentalism to more tolerance and less dogma until finally the early faith is quietly dropped altogether. In my understanding it is the same tree of faith with added rings. The styles of my faith may be different but I recognise in myself the same faith.

As Martin Luther King Jr said, 'Faith is the first step even when you don't see the whole staircase.' To me, 'faith' or 'trust' are words to describe the rubric underlying life: our meaning-making drive, if you like. To gain a sense of meaning, we need words and symbols to give shape to the profound mystery that we are to ourselves. I also openly acknowledge I have a particular faith alliance — the Christian faith — and this will be part of this book, of course. But faith and spirituality as concepts cover more than the particular and personal. They must be tested in all areas of life. They are tested in the ambiguity of power and ethical choices, and it is this larger faith dimension, and the questions it raises about all areas of life, be they personal, communal, political or global, that drives me.

There are three great imponderables: the universe, the self and the other. Faith opens up the possibilities to speak of these mysteries. We all need a faith story that makes sense of all three mysteries to understand why we are here and what it all means. Reason and science can only take us so far and must yield to myth to satisfy our hearts. As a child I devoured CS Lewis's *Chronicles of Narnia* and was lost in wonder when it was first read to me. Lewis spoke of his shift from atheism to Christian faith as a way of satisfying his longing for a hint of another world. His Christian friend JRR Tolkien taught him that, just as speech is an invention to describe objects and ideas, so myth is invention to understand truth.

But the faith breakthrough for Lewis came when Tolkien agreed with his rational scepticism that there are plenty of death and resurrection stories in Norse literature and Greco-Roman myths, and that there is nothing unique about the Christian story as it too is just myth. Tolkien replied that these stories in other times and other cultures are not untruths but fragments of light. He explained that such myths occur in different cultures and different times because they are fragments of the true Myth that speaks of God becoming human. This true Myth strangely resonated with the glimpses of intuition in the convinced atheist Lewis: intuition of another world, a deeper truth than the naturalistic or materialist world view of his atheism.

This true Myth also undergirds me as I seek to understand the universe, self and others.

PART I

Connection

Family values

Families are the great safety net throughout history. I suspect they are the true engines driving the progress of history. Parents everywhere make extraordinary sacrifices, often of their own happiness, just so that their children might have more opportunities and better lives. When I had children myself I finally fully appreciated the enormous sacrifices my parents made to raise me.

My father introduced me to faith in Jesus Christ at an early age. I trusted my father and knew intuitively that his faith was incredibly important to him and gave him strength.

He had a life-changing religious experience at eighteen. Although he was secretly baptised by his Catholic mother (which he only discovered in her latter years), his father hated religion and saw it as a source of trouble so the family never attended any church. My father's family were working class: his father was involved with under-the-radar SP gambling and the whole family were unquestioning Australian Labor Party–voting, Australian Rules football–mad, horse-racing punters. Both my father's uncles, who lived close by, were terrible alcoholics and rarely out of the pub.

My father's recreation as a young man was sport and dancing.

But he had to attend a monthly Presbyterian church service to qualify for the local church cricket team and, to his parents' surprise, one day he came home converted. The change was dramatic, and bewildering to all: he stopped drinking and attending Saturday night dances, dropped a lot of his old friends and started going to Bible classes and church.

After the war, during which he fought in Papua New Guinea, he studied at the Melbourne Bible Institute for two years. He went on under a returned soldier's scholarship to study at Melbourne University, where he did Ancient Greek and history; he ended up a schoolteacher by day as well as teaching Greek — the original language of the New Testament — to generations of students at his old Bible school in evening classes. He loved the Bible and when he said, 'the Bible says …', I knew what he really meant was, 'God says …'.

His conversion experience shaped my faith to trust in life-changing experiences. My father had been walking in one direction and, out of the blue, turned around to walk an entirely different path. It fitted with Bible stories like the Apostle Paul's experience on the Damascus road. I trusted my father, and so I trusted that people could be converted and could change.

I loved listening to my father teach the Bible. To him, the Bible was the indispensable arbiter of truth and sufficient in every area. He would advise, 'If people say the Bible is full of contradictions, just hand them one and say "show me". They never can.' I thought this was so tactically clever. But then one Sunday in his Bible class when I was thirteen years of age, I pointed out a contradiction that I had noticed. In the two conversion stories of Paul in Acts of the Apostles, there is a discrepancy about him hearing a voice. My father looked at it, and his red face told me to never question him like that. We never mentioned it again. I felt his shame, and it puzzled me, but I never doubted that his trust in God had totally changed his life.

My father was a loving authoritarian. He represented security, order and protection. We said grace at every meal and were not allowed to watch sport on television on Sunday or break the Sabbath. He presided over family devotions. He was a brilliant teacher, but the boundaries were very tight to avoid contamination from the world. Growing up in the swinging 60s, I knew that his first response to any request to venture beyond the boundaries was always, 'No'. As the oldest child, I was not even allowed to go to school dances because they were worldly. (Oddly enough, the rules changed for my brother and sister in following years.) But in the midst of his strong values I sensed we belonged to a different tribe from others, speaking a different language. It was as if I grew up bilingual and bicultural, switching between religious and secular language, which has been an asset in my later work in Africa and the US.

I was not surprised that my father agreed with Australia's participation in the Vietnam War and voted conservative. Conservative faith was the elixir of conservative politics. It represented order, security, and good, if paternalistic, governance. He had an expansive knowledge of history and politics but warned his sons off ever entering politics, saying it was dirty. The spiritual was pure.

Some years later in life, when his spiritual experience from his conversion had waned, our family observed his passion for the charismatic movement. This offered renewed contact with the supernatural through speaking in tongues, healings and words of prophecy as messages directly from God. He certainly never doubted the Bible and studied those parts of the New Testament that described similar experiences, but I realised that his deep search was not simply for Biblical truth but also for heart-warming spiritual experience.

Mum's faith was different. She sought understanding in literature and theatre and, though she trusted the biblical story, she sought a coherence and integration beyond it. These different subtleties in parental faith shaped me.

As a university student my Presbyterian-raised mother was recruited by the liberal modernist Student Christian Movement (SCM) to teach religious instruction at the nearby University High School. She was recruited because the Evangelical Union (EU) had so many volunteers, and the modernist SCM and the Bible-believing EU were bitter rivals. (Later I became the student president of the Monash University EU; my brother Peter and I were definitely on Dad's side of the faith ledger.)

My parents met in 1948 at a 'mixed' meeting of the tribes to organise the religious education teaching schedule at a neighbouring school. My mother, a novice, publicly asked, 'From what textbook will we be teaching the religion classes?' She remembers my father, an EU member, coming up and saying, 'I know a good teaching book.' She took out her notebook as he smiled and said, 'Yes. It's the Bible!'

That was all he needed. An unlikely romance began, crossing religious lines and shocking all their friends. When she was twenty, my mother survived what doctors had predicted would be a terminal illness. She was sick for two years with sub-acute bacterial endocarditis; her twenty-first birthday party was called off because she required hospitalisation. My father stayed loyal through her long illness, writing her letters every day. Despite her doctor telling my mother, when they learned she might survive, that she must never marry, my parents wed in a quiet morning ceremony in 1953. (It was a morning ceremony because my father's family insisted that they had to be at the Australian Rules football and horse races on a Saturday afternoon.)

My father prayed for her healing, but my mother was clear that it was medical science, in the form of penicillin and cortisone and the medical care of the wonderful Dr Ewen Downing, that saved her.

The medicos also told my mother that she must never even think of having children. As her first-born child, I was a miracle of prayer. (My mother also insisted that my middle name be Ewen, after her doctor. Her trust was never exclusive.)

My mother represented a broader faith that was accommodating to the world. Her first response to requests that ventured beyond the boundaries was always 'Yes!' and this made for some clashes in parenting. She read Germaine Greer and, in her own way, embraced feminism, going out to teach full time in the state system in the 1960s. Having a mother who had a university degree made me a rarity among my friends.

Mum read widely. She studied Freud (condemned then in most church circles) and would discuss his insights with us. I remember drawing a laugh when, at my twenty-first birthday, I thanked my father for teaching me Bible and my mother Freud. In a strongly teetotalling family she had a brandy bottle in the upper kitchen cupboard — just for the Christmas plum pudding, she told us. Oddly, the bottle had to be replaced regularly; but no, she insisted, she never drank.

All religions have a challenge in accommodating modernity and pluralism. Some are more open, with a dotted perimeter, but the fastest-growing are more suspicious and usually draw a hard boundary line of who is in and who is out. In Christianity they are of the 'the Bible says it and I believe it; so that settles it' variety. Faith is a boundary marker of identity and a protective fence against a hostile, changing world where nothing is sacred and everything is questioned. The gay marriage debate is really about fear that the institution of family is changing and is no longer sacred.

Humans need identity to function. In our family, Dad's faith was committed at the core and gave us a stable identity, while Mum's was open at the edges. This pendulum led to some big tensions, but also to a marriage that has survived sixty-three years.

One thing both parents did agree on was voting conservative. Mum was a classical liberal, identifying the freedom of the individual and conscience as the headstone in the arch of politics. She has been a lifelong member of the Australian Liberal Party. For Dad, the most important part of politics was security and order.

People are often perplexed that the political right can simultaneously own patriotism, militarism and individualism. How can a nation-state that often sacrifices the individual, be it through intrusive security laws or conscription to its wars, be the defender of individualism? That has never puzzled me, having grown up with my parents. Both those pieces of political architecture coexisted in their marriage. The missing piece in this equation, which I discovered through theological study, was social justice — which is usually owned by the political left.

Mum was never the submissive wife, and her independence taught us to deeply respect women. She took on full-time work teaching when all of her children were at school. This was unusual in her peer group of women in our church and neighbourhood. We attended the Baptist church as it was in walking distance, compared to the Blackburn Presbyterian Church. (This made a difference, as in the very early days of their marriage my parents did not own a car.) In the mid 70s our Baptist church was one of the first groups to open a women's refuge in a secret location to assist victims of domestic violence in the wider community. My early years in law included representing bashed and fearful women from this refuge. Often the work was literally lifesaving and liberating. But I also had extraordinary learning as a young lawyer not to always rush for court orders, as many returned with their children (against advice) to their husbands. Fear, shame and stigma meant they chose family identity over horrific violence and danger. This dilemma provoked anguish in a church that implicitly accepted patriarchy and submission by wives to their husbands, as taught by the Bible. In seeking to do the right thing in cases of domestic violence, were we sacrificing the God-ordained identity of the family and the authority of the Bible? For me, taking off the spectacles of a patriarchal culture and re-reading the sacred text was not hard, thanks to Mum. She pointed out that the first person to preach the good news was a woman. Mary Magdalene at the empty tomb on the first Easter Sunday was that woman, so she was the Apostle of apostles. So why were women not leaders and instead expected to be submissive to men?

We were brought up believing the Bible as the supreme authority in all matters. But our approach was anything but killjoy legalism. I remember the open-air Christmas plays our church organised when I was young: the safety of being held in my father's arms, feeling wonder with the angels singing, cattle bleating and the night stars shining. I learned when young how to speak in public and lead in youth groups and camps. I was given skills in a church setting that translated to leadership in secular domains. Sunday evening services were often turned into forums, with provocative current affairs questions and open discussions.

I never forgot the lesson that faith changes people. It had changed my father. I have never doubted that faith can change people's hearts and help them to deal with personal addictions, hard-heartedness and lust for power. From Mum I learned that faith was also relevant for the bigger issues, such as politics and psychology.

My life's work as it has unfolded has been about how faith addresses both the personal and impersonal, small and big, spiritual and social challenges. How it gives me nourishment for private struggles but addresses public battles for justice. So it is important to me that my faith addresses violence, racism, poverty and particularly the two issues that will dominate the next decade: climate change and the world's 60 million refugees.

It is why I have spent so much energy trying to defend Australian international aid, which funds our national response to the global effort on these two issues. Without such a response we ignore the reality that the world is a waterbed: too much unrelieved pressure overseas, although seemingly a long way from us, will mean that these pressures pop up in our faces.

Expect great things from God

For our secondary education my brother and I went to a Baptist school called Carey Grammar. Our father taught there for thirty-three years. The school has impressive alumni: an Australian test cricket captain, leading business tycoons, journalists, politicians, advertising gurus and, like most schools, an assortment of criminals now in jail.

I have continued to go back to school reunions when I can. They function a bit like that BBC television documentary that started as *Seven Up*. It tracks a group of British kids, interviewing them every seven years. As the years advance it is fascinating to see who is still strong in hope and resilience through life's vagaries: marriage breakdowns, mental illness, economic downturns and redundancy or bankruptcy.

Our school reunions are not as controlled an experiment as *Seven Up*; I have worked out that only those who feel positive about themselves and believe that they are somewhat successful bother to turn up. Life can be harsh, and who wants to be reminded of their past potential? Many do not want be judged by that standard.

I have observed at these reunions that it is not just the brightest or coolest at school that have 'made it'. Often it is the surprise packages no one at school seriously rated that have landed on their feet!

At the Carey school-year commencement service in 2015 it was this ambiguity of life and search for meaning I had in mind as I surveyed the packed crowd of parents, students and teachers in front of me. I felt a lot of nostalgia, as I had once been as wide-eyed and bushy-tailed as these young hopefuls staring up at me. I knew their parents were making huge sacrifices to pay $25,000 in school fees a year so that their children could get the best start in life. Some of these parents are rich, but many are not, working two jobs and overtime to keep their kids in that environment.

Most Carey students know something of the life of William Carey, after whom the school is named, and so I started there. He was a humble Baptist shoemaker in England who responded to a call he felt from God to become a missionary. A brilliant man with an extraordinary capacity to learn languages, he went to Bengal, India in 1793 and is known as the father of modern missions. He lived with the poorest people on earth. His son, Peter, died of dysentery, causing his wife, Dorothy, to suffer a nervous breakdown from which she never recovered. Despite her rages he refused to have her committed to an asylum back home, but cared for her until his death in Bengal. He translated the Bible into Bengali and wrote grammars of the Bengali and Sanskrit languages, preserving much ancient literature. His printing presses included forty-four other major languages and he is regarded as the preserver of Indian languages, such was his brilliance as a linguist. Many of these languages had never been printed before.

William Carey was also a huge promoter of social justice, protesting against caste tyranny and lobbying the governor general to put a stop to infant sacrifice and suttee. (Suttee, a custom where a woman was burnt alive on her deceased husband's funeral pyre, was rife until Carey's lobbying.) He also established schools and promoted education.

William Carey's motto, which we were taught at school, was 'Expect great things from God — attempt great things for God'. I told the crowd that this was a very fine sentiment but, given the expectations of parents paying expensive fees and the school's business model, which requires great academic results to attract future enrolment, was the motto now 'Expect great things for yourself — attempt great things for yourself'?

I myself have fallen into that same trap once or twice. It can be so easy to confuse temptation with calling, purpose and vocation. From 1993 to 1994 I had been mayor of St Kilda and loved the role. I did not want to go back to the small patch of being a minister in a local church. And it looked like I wouldn't have to. My career was shaping up beautifully: the Australian Democrats had offered me a senate seat in Federal Parliament and I could go straight in without even an election but as a casual vacancy. The temptation of politics had always been there and then, at age thirty-nine, it was being handed to me on a plate.

This had not yet been publicly announced and I was the speaker at a Christian Easter rally on Easter Sunday. Thousands were celebrating new life and their belief in resurrection in the streets of Melbourne and I was to address them from the steps of the State Parliament. But in my head I had already left being a minister and emotionally deserted this mob. As a politician I would need to build a much broader platform; being known as a minister of religion might even prove a barrier! I was now so focused on politics that I was mentally considering an identity makeover.

Then the person who introduced me to the crowd said some things that pierced my bubble and exposed this as temptation, not vocation. He said, 'Tim, we are proud of your faith and that you belong to us.' I looked down at the crowd of smiling faces and nodding heads and I thought with some arrogance and misgiving, 'But you don't realise that I am out of here.'

The man continued and said, 'We pray for you; you are our voice.'

I remember tears welling up in my eyes. These people were my mob. Who was I to decide they were all a bit too irrelevant for me to serve when I could have access to real power? Hadn't I set out on this vocation of Christian ministry with the affirmation of people like them? Had not my spirituality been nurtured in personally tough times by such people who loyally nurtured, cared for and prayed for me?

I look back now on this as a crossroads. It was the moment I realised that politics was my temptation but not my vocation and recovered a spirituality of humility and accountability. And I turned down the political seat! Temptation is not the same as vocation. True but not always obvious.

But back to Carey Grammar. Our current self-esteem culture dominates our world view and influences even great institutions like Carey Grammar School. It serves the myth that it's 'all about me'. All about my academic grades, my looks (must look good to feel good), my possession of the right brands and my success. My media advisor at World Vision had raised her kids in the Solomon Islands, as she is married to a Solomon Islander. She brought her kids back to a Melbourne private school for their secondary education and her children were shocked at how anxious and fretful their schoolmates became if they could not own a brand or product that no Solomon Islander would think necessary for life.

We are deceived if we do not live for something beyond ourselves and if we fall for the self-esteem myth as the goal. But it is so refreshing to discover those who are living beyond themselves. From the World Vision database we know that by far the greatest number of donors and greatest generosity in giving come from the poorest postcodes in Australia. People who know struggle seem to have more natural empathy for those who struggle — and they rarely expect to be recognised.

Another refreshing example of this willingness to live beyond oneself is a young Carey student called Hugh Evans, whom I had the honour of mentoring. He took to heart William Carey's motto. He spent time on Manila's infamous smoky mountain rubbish tip as a young ambassador for World Vision in the late 90s. This experience led him to start a youth development agency called Oaktree that is powering on in advocacy for the poor and is one of Australia's largest youth movements. Hugh went on to New York, where his global citizen organisation lobbies for greater aid to the world's poor. It runs an annual concert in New York's Central Park for 60,000 people. Speakers like President Modi of India and other prime ministers, as well as major international aid advocates such as Bono, have addressed it. In 2015 I also had the privilege to be on the platform and speak to the huge crowd as the sun set over the Manhattan skyline. In people like Hugh Evans we see that the drive to make a difference is well and truly alive in this generation.

Speaking of justice

When I completed school at Carey, I went on to Monash University where I studied law. My years of study and the subsequent few years of working in law caused me some consternation. While I loved arguing cases and fighting for people's rights, I also felt that justice was not always served — especially in matters pertaining to family law.

Furthermore, university life had introduced me to a breadth of political and social issues. Many Christians were taking strong stands against the Vietnam War. I began to question some of the assumed views of the Church as I knew it. I knew that justice was not always being served, and I had the growing realisation that justice was very important to my faith. These experiences seeded in me a strong desire to study theology in order to address my growing disquiet about the ways things were.

My idealistic approach is best illustrated in the poet Seamus Heaney's words:

> *History says*, Don't hope
> On this side of the grave,
> *But then, once in a lifetime*

The longed-for tidal wave
Of justice can rise up,
And hope and history rhyme.

But I have since learned that justice is complex. Amartya Sen in his book *The Idea of Justice* tells a story that I use in many of my speeches. Three children are fighting over who should have a flute. The first says, 'I should own it as I am the poorest and have no other toys. This would be my only toy.' The second child says, 'I should own it as I am the only one of the three of us who can play a flute.' The third child puts her case: 'Well, I should have it because I am the one who made this flute and after I finished making it you two turned up to claim what is mine.' Each of the three children stands for a different theory of justice and, while these competing theories are at the heart of so many of our big debates, we rarely disentangle or acknowledge them.

I naturally lean to the egalitarian argument of the poorest child. Next in order I am more sympathetic to the utilitarian argument of maximising happiness: giving it to the child who can actually use it. But when I ask audiences by a show of hands whom they think should have the flute, it is always overwhelmingly for the child who made the flute. For most it is a viscerally strong and ethically obvious lay-down misére. Of course they own it; how could you think otherwise? This neoliberal individual ownership argument is instinctively right to most people. In the middle are the utilitarians. Surely the one who can play it and maximise her pleasure and give the most pleasure to others makes the best recipient! Usually the poorest child comes in a distant last.

So why am I so out of step and where does my bias come from? It is my faith. I start with the belief that we are all only stewards for the ultimate Owner. If the only true property owner is God, then all that we think we own is not exclusively ours because we have used the world's resources to create them. Are not even the gifts and skills that allow us to create wealth God-endowed? If we are all God's children, then let us share a greater vision that includes the poor rather than just the 'obvious' ownership mentality. I acknowledge that ownership breeds incentive and reward, which are important for pride, purpose and growth, and a mindless socialism does not and never will work. A hand up is preferable to a hand out. (Interesting that in the Hebrew Scriptures farmers were told not to harvest their entire crop but to leave some gleanings for the poor. The poor were expected to harvest this themselves, thereby gaining the dignity of work and not just a handout.)

There is no question in my mind that we are failing at solving the great issues of the global commons (preservation of public goods like clean air and water and protecting living oceans and land). The challenges to the global commons are climate change, refugees and poverty — because we are too stuck on the granting of sole rights to the one who made the flute. Given vastly different talents and access, such an individual-ownership focus leads to gross economic inequality. The world is certainly already rich enough to feed, house and give dignity and work to all. How many houses or cars does a person need to keep the rain out and to move around? How much food does one person need when children are dying from starvation and malnutrition? How does asking those questions in a world of plenty raise the charge, 'So are you a socialist?' These questions merely focus on the strand of justice called fairness and point to the biblical vision that 'there shall be no poor among you'. Have we dismissed too casually the child who has no toy?

Fairness and diversity

In the charmed setting of a Swiss mansion, my tree of faith was stretched — adding a number of rings. It is strange to be poor in a rich nation, but at the time we were poor theological students. That experience of often not being able to afford a meal out and having to think twice about even buying a coffee has reminded me that poverty is always relative to those around you.

When Merridie and I were there in the early 1980s, studying theology in an international student community, Switzerland was just starting to face an awful truth: that, in protecting their neutrality in World War II, they had closed their borders to many Jews. The secret emerged while we were there that an estimated 25,000 died when they could not cross into a neutral country and were left to the Nazis. Swiss nationalism was strong and as we arrived patriots had firebombed and blown up the first McDonald's in Zurich. (It was seen as a symbol of American imperialism.) We observed the treatment of foreigners, then Slavic and Italian, who were given temporary passes to do the dirty jobs such as cleaning the trains and roads in winter. They were despised and enjoyed few rights. Our first child was born there and the hospital system was magnificent, but we never forgot the experience of not being fluent in any of the major languages of Switzerland and feeling alone. We did not understand much and at times felt vulnerable.

The smallest kindnesses shown to us by a Swiss national were overwhelming when we felt so invisible. But it meant that we were becoming much more open at the edges. The role reversal, from being secure as an Australian in Australia to becoming a foreigner, made me read my Bible differently.

While we theology students all shared a Christian faith and were training for the Baptist ministry, it was challenging to live in a community for four years with more than twenty-five other nationalities. There were Africans, a Palestinian who was born in Nazareth, a Russian, Americans, Japanese, an Indonesian, Latinos, Nigerians and many Europeans, including Brits. More important than the theology was the interaction. The American Baptists paid the bills and we regarded them as nice, but naive to think that bankrolling the seminary meant their way should prevail in Europe.

One of the big culture clashes we experienced involved the Italians. They were a large group in the student body and ate lunch together and had wonderful loyalty as a tribe. When it came to exams, if the lecturer left the room their socialism became practical as they would start sharing answers and discussing the questions in Italian in front of the rest of us who had diligently prepared. The British, German, Scandinavian, American, and Aussie and Kiwi students were all massively offended by the Italians' cheating! We could turn a blind eye to the Slavic students running dubious side businesses out of school hours, selling second-hand cars as new, but cheating in exams was a breach of the social contract! Our Italian colleagues were shocked that we called it cheating: it was solidarity with the weaker students.

These fault lines were my first insight into an issue that would dominate my later work. Those of us who were outraged belonged to contract societies, but most of the world belongs to family/clan/tribal societies. For Australians and northern and western Europeans, unlike for southern and eastern Europeans, we accept the social contract that if we all play by the same transparent rules our families will all be better off. We pay our taxes and we all get education, health facilities, roads and a social safety net. But for tribal cultures, you trust no one outside the clan. Why would you pay your taxes if those at the top have a duty to just look after their own clan, tribe or family first?

It's the same concern in both societies — to protect our own families — but totally different approaches. Universal and transparent governance runs counter to clan nations' instincts and experience. Corruption is the result.

And now, contract societies are in crisis. The bailout of the big financial institutions in 2008 by taxpayers, while the same taxpayers lost their homes, is a breach of the social contract. Only one banker went to prison and many of the other banking executives still got their bonuses. All this when 6 million poorer Americans lost their homes and 8 million lost their jobs through this corruption on Wall Street!

The regular revelations that rich people and big corporations such as Google and Starbucks are not paying tax have frayed the belief that we are all playing by the same rules. The hacking of files in just one legal firm in Panama, Mossack Fonseca, has shown us that the rich in 'contract' societies are just as greedy and corrupt when it comes to avoiding their share of the tax burden as the rich in 'clan' societies.

These are the fault lines I encountered in my first exams at the seminary. In that interplay all the students started to become global citizens, as we were all outsiders and had to learn to listen and bend our preferred styles. And yes, learn it in Switzerland — a putative contract nation, but one that was the belly of the beast of international tax avoidance. We all banked at Credit Suisse, founded in 1885, as students, which was in 2014 found guilty of aiding and abetting tax evasion and fined $2.6 billion.

I now believe that it is impossible to understand your faith until you experience living out of your own culture. Your blind spots are only addressed when you realise how your perspective on truth is determined by your own culture and experiences.

I was elected student president after my first year (Australians are not a threat to anyone) and had to face an explosive financial issue. Most students were subsidised by a paid work scheme, which helped maintain the seminary property and run things like the book shop and English classes. On top of the paid work was a small scholarship. But some students owned cars, which was regarded as a luxury in those days. With some tightening of seminary finances due to American donors reducing their grants, a resolution was passed that only students without a car could qualify for a scholarship. Fair enough?

Not quite. Students who owned cars pointed out that, though they owned a car, they never ate meat, bought far fewer books than others and saved money by not going home during summer break, while those who were 'poor' because they did not own a car did all those things. How fair was this resolution?

In addition, some of the paid work was more highly valued. As the English teacher in the seminary I only had to work half the hours for the same pay as the students in the gardening crew. How were we all equal? It certainly sensitised me to inequality in a world where CEO remuneration is out of all kilter to any norm and sixty-one individuals own as much wealth as 3.5 billion of the poorest inhabitants on this planet, while we are told to trust what an impartial market values as the price of freedom.

It was an agonising process as the student president to try to determine whether equality was achievable, even though it was something we were in principle all committed to achieving. It was a foretaste of the complexities of social policy and welfare that have occupied my later life.

Committed at the core
but open at the edges

The Sunday evening communion service at my first church in St Kilda was often a testing time. We had some very committed lifelong Christians who were at times uncomfortable with the numerous homeless people who were attending. The homeless people (somewhat understandably) could not always get their personal hygiene together; some were drug addicted and others were mentally ill. During the service some would walk out for a smoke and come back in.

One evening as we began to prepare for the communion an older man who had just turned up publicly asked whether he could participate. We assured him that as long as he believed in Jesus he was welcome.

He then said, 'But I've just been in prison because I've done some bad things.' We replied that we have all done bad things and at this table no one is superior or inferior: we are all sinners in need of grace.

One of our Aboriginal church members, who had been brought up in a Christian orphanage and been taught some strict rules, said, 'Hang on minute: you can't if you've had sex before marriage.' The man looked taken aback.

He said, 'Well, that rules me out. But where does that leave everybody else here?' As he glanced around the gathered congregation I saw a lot of people suddenly get itchy eyebrows and start studying the floor. Embarrassment was setting in, and this was not how a sacred moment is meant to run. So I intervened, saying, 'We are all sinners and no one is anything but a flawed human here tonight.' I reminded them that God alone judges, so we had better not assume divine pretensions by finger-pointing. As the cup, in this case a glass of watery grape juice, was handed around the congregation the ex-convict took his turn. He drained it and said loudly, 'Not bad!' as if it were fine shiraz. Acceptance and grace is smoother than the finest wine; he was included!

To build such a community our motto was 'committed at the core and open at the edges'. To have real mission we needed to be committed to the way of Jesus; but his way was open to those in Palestine who were unclean and despised, because Jesus taught that God loves them. Communion, or the Eucharist, is at the centre of this. We eat the bread from one loaf and drink from one cup, even with people we may not like or cannot stand. Jesus indeed shared that last supper, on which the Eucharist is modelled, with one he knew would shortly betray him and another who would soon deny even knowing him.

The act of communion says there are no distinctions of superior or inferior with God; we can find community and still not demonise others. As beneficiaries of the Eucharist bread and wine we are embraced by God, but as recipients of this divine acceptance we are made into God's agents of reconciliation. The forgiveness we have received must be offered to others, even to strangers or our enemies. This helps stop the endless attempts to justify why 'I have a right to my hurt' and why 'I have a right to my hatred'. It is why repentance and communion means a radical change.

A song of strength

One of the most brilliant colleagues I have had at World Vision was the former global manager of Boston Consulting. He worked for us as the World Vision International COO for seven years while still living in Boston. His passion and superb consulting skills were quite a mix in one man. I was intrigued and asked him how this had come about. He told me about a formative experience he had as a young man on his first trip to Africa, well before he became a consultant.

He was miles out in the African bush, many hours from the main city, bumping along in the tray of a truck. The road had potholes big enough to swallow trucks, so every mile was bone-jarring and keenly felt and the speed was mesmerisingly slow. Suddenly the truck stopped dead in the thick bush. They all jumped out and immediately saw the problem. A huge tree had fallen across the road. Sitting atop the massive trunk was a lonely local with a tiny axe, forlornly chipping away. Those from the truck saw that his puny effort was a hopeless solution to the blockage and got out some chains and tried to wrap them around the tree trunk. But it was so massive they could not get the chains around. After scratching their heads they agreed that it could only be moved through human effort. So, with shoulders to the tree, after the count of three, they tried to move it. It barely shuddered, let alone moved. Another vehicle coming from the opposite direction had stopped as it too could not get around the blockage. They too got out and put their shoulders to the trunk, but it barely groaned. Suddenly, even though they were in the bush miles from anywhere, locals started appearing. They had no idea where the locals had come from or how they'd heard about the blockage, but there they were.

Even with all these extra bodies and bulging muscles, the trunk was just a dead weight; it all looked completely impossible. The depressing reality of two hours of bone-jarring journey back from where they had just come seemed inescapable. Someone said, 'Well, let's not die wondering, so they got ready for one more go. My colleague remembers putting his shoulder to the trunk for this futile last shove. He remembered seeing a frail elderly man who had just staggered out of the bush shoulder up next to him. He remembers because he looked at him and thought, 'Fat lot of help you'll be. Frail, elderly and weak.'

But this man began to sing a song. The Africans had not been responding to the count of three, but waited for a refrain in the song as their signal. As the old man hit a crescendo in his song the locals instantly knew to heave. Amazingly, the tree shifted a half centimetre. They took a breather and reassembled. This time my colleague and the Europeans were ready as the old man began his chant; on the refrain they heaved and this formerly immoveable dead weight shifted another half centimetre. So this elderly man sang and they heaved, rested, sang and pushed forty to fifty times and, inch by inch, after hours of sweaty singing, they had moved it just enough for the trucks to squeeze through and continue on their journey.

For my colleague, this was a profound lesson for his future as a consultant. The mission never changed: it was to shift this obstacle. The strategies were analysed and the least effective quickly discarded: axes and chains wouldn't work so brute effort was the best, indeed only, realistic strategy. But even with the best strategy to achieve the mission there was no progress. So what changed? What changed was a frail elderly man's song. With his song he was able to reach into their hearts and find a force that did not seem to be there before. His song seemed to magically bring them into alignment and release power that achieved the mission. Human alignment around a purpose is not just a productivity strategy for greater profit. It is a social and national strategy. Every successful team sport knows it's the key, as do vibrant communities.

Great leaders find a song that overcomes misalignment, frustration and wasted energy when our wheels are spinning. They reach into our hearts with a vision — a story — a clarity that unleashes what was not there before. How we hunger for leaders like that and long to pick up the strains of that tune. Where are those leaders today? Leaders with the imagination and courage (the two most important attributes of leadership) to do something different and take us to a new place? Locally I have seen leaders like that. But most leaders in Western democracies are so timid that they commission polls and focus groups and think leadership means interpreting what people want. We perish for lack of vision.

Of course, not any song will do. It must resonate with our deepest heart hungers and speak to our souls, and echo our intuitions about meaning.

The solutions are staring you in the face

One of the humblest and most committed members of staff at World Vision Australia is Tony Rinuado. He had been working in Niger as an agriculturalist for years. He was feeling discouraged, as the trees planted at great government expense to retard erosion and give poor farmers a better yield were dying. It takes a lot of work and expense to plant a tree and keep it alive.

He was changing a flat tyre and looking at the surrounding lunar landscape of dust and dead tree stumps. (Trees in Niger are cut down for firewood, as it is the main energy source for cooking.) In despair, he prayed. He believes God spoke to him. He noticed that the nearest stump had a little bit of shrub growing — not unusual, and something normally burnt away by farmers because it is surface fluff. But then he saw it differently. That greenery suggested that this useless stump was not dead. Those strands of greenery suggested a root system that was still alive. As he noticed many other stumps with some bushy outgrowth, he realised this meant there was an underground forest there that he had never seen.

Staring him in the face was such a simple solution. He developed a low-cost, simple technology plan to re-green the nation. He taught poor farmers that the solution was in their pocketknife or machete, which they all owned. Instead of clearing away this growth or burning it, as was the practice, they were to prune it and watch what happened. Dig a trench around the stump to catch any precipitation, choose just the best stems shooting out, and cut the others away. Revisit regularly and cultivate them on the stump. Be patient and watch a miracle unfolding! Since it was a difficult environment for the seedlings to grow in, those trees with established root systems had a much better chance at survival. The genius of Tony's solution was to work on the trees that already had roots, rather than starting from scratch with seedlings.

Thanks to Tony's Farmer Managed Natural Regeneration (FMNR), there are now 5 million hectares of new trees in Niger. From outer space satellites you can see the dramatic difference pre-Tony and post-Tony. *The Guardian* deemed it the third most significant intervention in Africa in the last decade! And it is poor farmers doing it themselves, on their own small plots, and taking control of their lives. It is not a top-down massive government program, and it is so cheap.

This technique of Tony's is spreading throughout the rest of Africa and now in Indonesia, India and other parts of Asia. It is one of the best things World Vision does. In 2014 I watched Tony's work in barren Ethiopia, which had been one of the poorest areas where World Vision works. People were abandoning villages where their ancestors had lived for millennia. For Tony's workshop we had bussed in poor farmers from a wide catchment area to a place that only a few years earlier had been denuded and devastated. It was now blooming thanks to FMNR and Tony's training. There were orchards and vegetable gardens and water storage plans with elevated catchment pools, and the community was thriving.

It was not just the emotion of watching Tony lead these amazed farmers from site to site to demonstrate the techniques — it was the emotion watching farmers in the area explaining to their neighbours how they now farmed between the trees and how they had turned around a local catastrophe. It was even more the emotion of seeing the ripple effects in saving culture and history. This area had some of the oldest Christian churches in the world — carved into rock faces some 1700 years ago — and they are still central in worship and community life. People's cultural and religious history was being abandoned as they lost trees because it meant the loss of rainfall (deforestation can cause changes in precipitation), the loss of animals and the loss of soil fertility. As an Aussie I was proud to see both the local variety of acacia and our West Australian acacia trees being introduced. Its seed can be ground into a wheat paste and nourish people through the hungry months. A fertiliser and food tree to boot.

To witness poor communities now surviving the hungry months of the year because they have better crops, and to see their pride that they have re-greened their land, improved crop yield, and done all this without costly fertilisers and tractors and expensive technology, is to witness renewed morale and stronger community.

Thank God Tony saw that bit of brush on the tree stump staring him in the face!

In the company of saints

My wife's aunt Lilian was Scottish. She met her husband, Howard, my wife's uncle, when they were both young missionaries in China before Mao and the Communists threw all the missionaries out in 1949. Aunt Lily prayed and she encouraged and she took an interest in us. I was impressed to know that she was a personal friend of Eric Liddell (of *Chariots of Fire* fame, and one of my heroes) and exuded the same serving spirit and principled life as he did.

Aunt Lily was also funny. At her 100th birthday celebrations, my wife said, 'Aunt Lily, Tim is also celebrating a birthday next week. He'll turn fifty.'

Lily looked at me with great concern and, with the slightest of twinkles in her eye, said, 'Oh my, you are getting on!'

Aunt Lily had lost her first babies — twin daughters — in China, and they were buried there. But she stayed there, in those demanding circumstances, to fulfil the calling that had drawn her out of her sheltered life back home. We were amazed at her commitment. Was she just unusually tough or driven? No; she had a purpose, and it transfigured suffering even in her terrible loss. She grieved but never allowed herself to become resentful.

Eric Liddell cared for all the missionaries, foreigners and prostitutes alike, as well as all the children in the camp where he was interned by the Japanese when they invaded China in 1937. Eric worked in the same spirit as Aunt Lily. And like Lily he suffered for his calling. Eric ended up dying after becoming ill in the camp. But he died strong in his faith and remaining a man of prayer, simplicity and purpose. He'd had the world at his feet as an Olympic champion but chose to teach and serve the poor in China. While at the camp, Eric broke his own strict rules for keeping the Sabbath and not participating in Sunday sport. He saw that the children in the camp desperately needed some play and hope, so he organised and ran the Sunday sporting games. This is the man who gave up a gold medal because he would not run his best event on the Sabbath.

Of course, the Sabbath as a day of rest was all about sustainability: one day a week animals and humans were to be rested. A Sabbath of years after seven years required agricultural land to lie fallow, giving it a chance to restore itself. A Sabbath of years was also the time all debts were to be forgiven; this financial Sabbath sustained the poor, allowing them to start afresh and have hope.

Eric came to recognise that Sabbath legalism did not give life; the Sabbath was made to serve humans and sustain children in awful circumstances of internment. Prayer changes us even if it is hard to see if it changes the world!

I have often mused on the lives of people like Eric Liddell and Aunt Lily whose faith led them to go to

China. It was the big missionary cause of the early 1900s and hundreds of dedicated young Christians undertook language and Bible training to prepare for years of hard work in the cities and outposts of China. In those days China was seen as a poor and backward pagan monolith — only of interest to missionaries and a few traders.

Today, of course, China has become the economic and military powerhouse of the world. It scouts out economic opportunity all over the developing world and is one of the biggest contributors to aid and development in Africa. It also sends its young people out to all corners of the globe for education and training. My sister and her husband have had seven Chinese students board with them over the last six years or so, and my parents took in a Chinese Malaysian girl while she studied at university.

Now many Australians resent that our economy is so utterly dependent on China's rise (and fall) as it is our biggest trading partner. But paradoxically China, still a communist and atheist state, is experiencing a phenomenal growth of religion. In fact Chinese Christians may already outnumber US Christians. Who would have predicted China would become the largest Christian nation on earth? Much of this growth has happened through the grassroots explosion of what are called house-churches, which evolved from the Bible training and church-planting that pre-dated the Communist revolution.

The faithful work of humble believers like Aunt Lily and Eric Liddell back in the early part of the 1900s has provided an inspiring answer to a nation's hunger for something beyond a materialistic culture.

The atheists of Melbourne

I have an atheist university colleague, Dick Gross, who some years ago wrote a fascinating book called *The Godless Gospel*. He succeeded me as mayor in the city of St Kilda (by then amalgamated into Port Phillip). His book is not at all an attack in the manner of the secular fundamentalists like Richard Dawkins; far from it. He laments that, in being unable to believe, he and his children miss out on the finest things religion provides. He believes there needs to be a substitute for atheists, such as regular community gatherings with singing, a parallel Sunday school for atheist kids, a weekly offering bowl and a ritual that meditates on beauty, mystery and meaning — all without God. He rang me after his book was published and asked me if I could set up some speaking engagements in churches to promote his book. I was stunned and suggested that churches might not be his best forum. I was more stunned when he said that, on the contrary, churches were the only places he was able to get a hearing as his atheist crowd were all too uninterested and disorganised.

I am fascinated that there is now a group of rationalists, including atheists, who meet each month on a Sunday in Melbourne for what they call Sunday Assembly. It was started after an advertisement in London invited people to turn up for this novel experiment model and it took off. There has been a burgeoning number of such meetings in London. Kate, a young friend of my daughter's, leads the one in Melbourne. And it seems very inclusive as Father Bob McGuire, a Catholic priest, and I, although a reverend, are on their invite list. I sense that they are groping for a post-secular spirituality, not atheism. Kate told me that she had withdrawn from the community for a time because putting out the chairs, leading and organising the gatherings always fell on the same few. I reminded her that the best things are hard, and look at the results if you persevere.

When I spoke there it was just like a religious worship service, beginning with a welcome, an offering and sharing news from the community, followed by silence and reflection and a secular sermon. A number of members wore t-shirts reading 'atheist, rational and evidence-based is my belief'. And yes, there was congregational singing. Kate, who was the 'worship leader' that morning, explained that as rationalists and an exclusively evidence-based congregation, we sing because science has shown that group singing releases endorphins and these are very good for our health. We sang Paul McCartney's 'Let it Be' and some Carol King and the endorphins were soon raging! I spoke about my faith and asserted that we all live by faith. Surprisingly there was much warmth and agreement with what I said. There was an unmistakable spirituality among these atheists and rationalists seeking a non-faith spirituality, and I commend them.

Self-respect

The Transit soup kitchen is a street outreach that feeds people who have known unemployment, illness and homelessness. Just after I returned from Nepal after the horrific earthquake that had killed 8000 Nepalese in May 2015, I received a donation of $200 for earthquake relief. The money was given by the people coming to Transit for a free meal.

One of the donors was Susan Kye, a fifty-eight-year-old woman who had raised three children with a husband in prison and little cash. She lives in government housing and is recovering from depression. She gave the last few dollars in her purse, saying, 'It's nice to know you can do something for someone else, no matter what your circumstances are … There is always something you can do. I've got it pretty good compared to other people.'

Louise, a survivor of domestic violence, spoke as her two fair-haired daughters climbed over her. She said that she wanted to teach her kids about the importance of aid. 'I want my kids to know there is no shame in receiving aid when you need to ask for it, but I don't want them growing up thinking they can put their hand out and the world owes them.'

I loved the insight of fifteen-year-old Dairna Irwin, who lives in a caravan and picks up food at Transit for her ill mother. She said only poor people could understand the challenges facing those in desperate situations. 'Wealthy people may give, but it is rare. And people who are less fortunate — like the people here — it's more likely that they would offer money because they actually know what people are going through, unlike wealthy people. Often they don't know what people here, or the people in Nepal, are going through.'

Self-interest or
shared interest?

A famous Australian politician, Jack Lang, is reported to have quipped that 'in a two-horse race, always back the horse called self-interest'. Most of us would agree.

Grill'd is a healthy burger chain doing well in Australia. Its service is much slower than Hungry Jacks', its prices are higher, and its food comparably nutritious, but it is winning customers. It is not exactly part of the slow-food movement, but it's offering an alternative to choosing food solely by the criteria of speed and low price.

My son Elliot's charity, YGAP, runs a social enterprise restaurant in inner Melbourne called Feast of Merit. (It is named for a tradition from Nagaland in north-east India. In Naga culture, when you become rich — meaning you have a lot of pigs and bags of rice — you can choose to throw a feast of merit. This means hosting a party for the whole village, particularly the poor, and that might go on for two weeks or a month — whatever time it takes to liquidate all your assets. When everything is gone, you have a glorious gold cloak placed on your shoulders in a ceremony of great respect. Then you start again with nothing — except for your gold cloak. I witnessed this ceremony and love the cultural insight that we bring nothing into this world and take nothing with us; so wealth is to bless people, especially the poor, now.)

All the profits from the Feast of Merit restaurant go to YGAP's work to support local impact entrepreneurs in some of the world's toughest communities. YGAP has branched out to support young entrepreneurs both in Australia and the developing world, focusing on the need for business to solve social and environmental problems in addition to making profits.

When the property next door to the Feast of Merit restaurant came up for lease, YGAP imagined using it to set up a shopfront and a co-working space for social entrepreneurs. It would be the natural extension for the restaurant to invest in hope. But the landlord was not interested, as some other commercial outlet was offering much more rent.

Through some circuitous means they found out this 'other commercial outlet' was Grill'd. Young people know no bounds to their idealism, and so they contacted a member of the Grill'd executive team to explain their vision and why they needed the site. Of course the estate agent wanted Grill'd as a tenant; even if YGAP could offer more, he wouldn't lease to a not-for-profit without a hefty guarantee.

Disappointed but undeterred, they somehow got the ear of the CEO of Grill'd, who said he agreed that, despite Grill'd raising money for charities at every outlet, they should be doing more. He decided to help. Grill'd withdrew their offer and helped YGAP secure the property. The head of the Grill'd property team went on to offer my son support with reviewing the agreement and helping with the guarantee. Now *that* is the business of business. Grill'd have since gone down the street and leased a more expensive site, but they feel they have made the right decision because excessive profits do not have to always trump social good.

There may not be many Grill'ds in this world, but the notion of shared value, not share price or stock value, is taking root. It is the beguilingly simple idea that you can make a profit and simultaneously aim to solve social challenges. Indeed that is the true purpose of business. How refreshingly different in these times when we are told that a CEO is entitled to rewards 400 times the average salary of one of his employees. Here is a blueprint for seeing if businesses will do their part for the common good.

Now at the new space taken over by Feast of Merit, Merridie and I, with others, run a monthly Sunday night celebration called Feast of Spirit. It is for young people who have everything but who long for faith and spirituality. The hunger for spirit in this land of plenty is more pressing than the marvellous food being served next door in the restaurant. Humans cannot live by bread alone.

PART II

Love thy neighbour

The old gods

Trust and loyalty are easy when it comes to family and friends; but they are tested when it comes to neighbours who are neither. Hunter-gatherers lived in small groups of up to 150 people. Anthropologists have theorised this is because you could know and trust a mob up to around that number. Trust was critical: if your tribe failed you, your life was at risk.

With the breakthrough of settled agriculture and domesticating animals, larger populations could be fed and organised to cohabit. Now not everyone had to hunt or prepare food and so people could specialise, freeing up human activity for art, architecture, learning, law and medicine. We owe the ensuing explosion in human knowledge and progress to this specialisation and the communication that was enabled by writing.

From small citadels defending agricultural lands, eventually cities grew, keeping much larger numbers of people in close proximity to each other. How do you trust larger groups when the time-honoured method of gossip cannot cover everyone? How can you tell who is a solid citizen and who's a thief and freeloader? Religion was the main way to make the jump: common beliefs and trust in the same gods produced a stamp of assurance that these unknown others were still on our side and could be trusted.

Religious trust is still with us today, even after the development of the nation-state. There are essentially three main options for a nation to settle the issue of trust of the neighbour within its borders: religious nationalism, ethnic nationalism, or a secular nationalism that aims at pluralism and fosters trust through the universal rule of law and treating everyone equally.

Religion is such a powerful force of loyalty and trust that we have seen it create nations. In modern times Pakistan was the first, in 1947, but at the cost of a split in Punjab and Kashmir as Muslims fled north to the new Pakistan, and Hindus and Sikhs fled south to India. The religious violence that was largely contained before Indian independence in 1948 suddenly exploded as national boundaries were drawn. In Pakistan all but Muslims fled the Islamic state as religious tensions were inflamed by religious nationalism. Partition was horrific and millions died. Border violence continues to sporadically flare today.

Religious nationalism is evident in the Sunni majority in Saudi Arabia vying with the Shia theocracy of Iran. Both are flexing their muscle for dominance in the Middle East, particularly in Iraq and Syria. The catastrophe of Syria is largely the result of a proxy war between these religious nations, with Russia and Iran backing President Assad of Syria, and the West backing Saudi Arabia and the Syrian rebels seeking to depose Assad. Some 8 million Syrians are internally displaced within their own nation. Three hundred thousand are dead (including

15,000 children) and 1 million have fled to Europe. The cost of religious nationalism is becoming unbearable as it threatens to swamp Europe with refugees.

Ethnic nationalism is also tricky. In nations like Fiji the 'sons of the soil' overthrow democratic governments that elect Indians who are not of the proper ethnic pedigree. There is a similar story in Malaysia, which preferences the Malay-born in university entrance and government employment. Historically this marginalised those not born to Malay parents and in the past has seen anti-Chinese race riots express the ethnic chauvinism against local Chinese business success. Israel is another example; though democratic, its citizenship is based on birth to a Jewish mother. There are sponsored birthright tours for Jews born outside Israel, whose families have never lived in Israel, to remind them of their right of return because of Jewish blood. And Palestinians who are Israeli and whose families go back millennia in the land feel that they are second-class citizens in their own nation.

The secular state is struggling to define its identity. Some nations, like Japan, are secular but resolve difference by refusing to embrace it. There is virtually no immigration and so Japanese homogeneity is maintained. But it comes at great economic cost as the economy and population stagnate. Immigration is critical for economic growth and renewal. For this reason most other nations have accepted skilled migration and attempted to teach an ethic of respect for difference.

Secular nations embrace multiculturalism, believing that cultural identity can be separated from the country of origin by offering newcomers state support and legislation to protect them. It is a magnificent attempt to foster respect for minority cultures. The assumption that I applaud is that, if migrants are respected and taught the host nation's liberal values of pluralism and social democracy, they will integrate. Mostly this has proven true. In the US just about everyone has a hyphen: Hispanic-American, African-American, Irish-American, Jewish-American, Chinese-American and Muslim-American. Indeed, thanks to multiculturalism, the US and Australia have far less Islamist terrorism and far greater integration than Europe, with its Muslim ghettoes. When I hear Europeans lamenting that multiculturalism has failed I am astounded because I think they have never really tried to implement social and economic policies that celebrate difference along with economic integration and citizenship. For example, it is still apparent that Germans speak of 'German Turkish–speakers', not 'Turkish-Germans'.

So ethnic nationalism is on the rise in European secular nations from Poland to Hungary. A softer form of this is evident in Scottish independence and now the UK Brexit referendum compensating for the bloodlessness of secularism and satisfying tribal identity needs. Immigration and the fear of the European and Muslim migrant is a real force driving the Brexit. Same with parties such as Reclaim Australia, the UK Independence Party, the Black Shirts in Hungary and Greece, the National Front in France and the Tea Party in the US; all these suggest problems ahead for the Western pluralist multicultural project. They offer a spirituality of soil and blood — the old gods — and pose dangerous answers to identity.

Tribalism puts the brain into neutral as it sweeps up the emotions of belonging. Tribal politics in Africa are endemic and in places like Kenya they cost lives at every election. The great achievement of former Tanzanian president Julius Nyerere was to teach the forty tribes of Tanzania to primarily identify themselves as Tanzanians, not tribes. This literally saves lives every election. In Papua New Guinea, which has 18 per cent of the world's languages, tribalism bedevils politics. Tribe ('Wontok') is trusted rather than fairness in national policies, and politicians play to that, doling out largesse to their clan rather than insisting that we can transcend tribalism and learn to trust an impartial national safety net. Of course, once a year they do transcend the local as the citizens of Papua New Guinea divide into either Blues or Maroons to watch the Australian Rugby League State of Origin rugby match between New South Wales and Queensland. And every year people die from the fighting that erupts between Blues and Maroons over a televised game in another nation!

I favour the secular pluralist state, because religious and ethnic difference are exclusive, intolerant and trigger conflict. They lack a spirituality underpinning respect for the other. But legislating respect and anti-discrimination laws is only a stopgap measure. When such laws fail to be credible or unite us, we resentfully turn to other common denominators such as caste, class, race and ideology, but particularly to flag-waving nationalism.

Under the gaze

In early 2013 I was coming out of Gaza where I had been working with World Vision. My time there had been harrowing. The Israeli blockade by sea and land has reduced it to the biggest open-air prison on earth. The tunnels into Egypt, once their lifeline, have been closed by President el-Sisi, the new military leader who threw out the democratically elected Morsi from the Muslim Brotherhood. So in Gaza the basics for life are restricted and unemployment is rife. So few of the necessities to rebuild shattered homes after the war are getting through to Gaza. A trickle of Palestinians needing medical care is sometimes allowed out for treatment in Israel. In the queue behind me were some Palestinian women and their children.

We had walked the kilometre-long concrete tunnel of no-man's-land and were through to the fortress in the security building for border checks. Above me, looking down through the glass, were Israeli soldiers with guns. A female soldier grabbed the microphone and asked what was under my pants on my left knee. I explained it was a knee bandage supporting my knee due to an old football injury. She demanded that the bandage come off and be put through the security belt. I explained that, in my trendy tight chinos, I could not achieve this without taking off my pants. She shouted, 'Well, take your pants off!'

I said, incredulous, 'What, right here in front of these women and children?' She said yes — and she had the gun! The women in the queue looked shocked as I made gestures trying to prepare them that I was going to pull down my pants.

There I stood in my less-than-trendy underpants, waiting, while these Muslim women in hijabs and burqas shielded their children's eyes. Then a male soldier, who had not seen or heard this exchange, shouted at me: 'What do you think you are doing?'

I pointed to the guard who had commanded me to take my pants off. He ignored her and said, 'You cannot take your pants off here! Put them on.'

The embarrassment and powerlessness I felt as I struggled to squeeze back into my tight chinos is minor compared to the daily border harassments Palestinians suffer. I just had to face my wife back home, whose first comment was, 'Yeah, but were your underpants clean?'

The stranger as the scapegoat

Israel is the world's exemplar of the challenge to live together when we are strangers. Jews have been persecuted through history and treated as the alien 'other'. I get distressed when I see security guards at every Jewish school and synagogue in my safe, stable hometown, Melbourne. I know anti-Semitism is on the rise again, and it is an irrational ancient hatred. I understand why my Jewish friends insist that they need a strongly defended Jewish homeland — Israel — so they can retreat behind its borders under the law of return quickly if needed because, even in Australia, things can sour with little warning.

At a large conference held in Melbourne for the world's religions I was on a panel compèred by Australian Broadcasting Corporation journalist Geraldine Doogue. It was being filmed for television. In the spirit of tolerance befitting the conference, with over 10,000 delegates from all faiths, the panel included a Jewish rabbi, a Saudi Muslim woman, a Buddhist and me. We were all bending over backwards to find common ground without denying our faith. Did we believe in the same God? Were all our faiths aiming for a better world with a common ethic? Were we all equally respectful and why did we treat others as *dhimmi* or infidels? It was all charming until our Saudi panellist dropped a disgusting anti-Jewish bombshell to the effect that Jews were all greedy, bad people. The rabbi from Norway did not even blink; he was so accustomed to these attitudes. The conversation quickly moved on. After the event Geraldine and I talked about it and agreed we both just froze in shock at what we had heard. I said I felt bad I hadn't said something there and then, and she reproached herself for not pulling up the Muslim woman. Of course, this comment was edited out of the televised version. Later in the week I went to a Sabbath dinner in a Jewish home with the Norwegian rabbi present, so I profusely apologised for my silence. He thanked me and merely shrugged. This indicated to me that it was not an exceptional experience for him.

Interactions like this cannot be edited out of real life. It was precisely these attitudes that led to the Holocaust. They were embedded in Christian Europe and exploited by the Nazis. On the whole, Jews had actually survived better under Islamic authorities, from Baghdad to Spain, than under Christian rule. But not now. There are, according to a best guess, maybe fewer than twenty Jews in Baghdad and a few thousand in Tehran, all too old to leave, when both cities once had thriving communities. Many Islamic states have been infected with anti-Semitism. Blood libel and racist caricatures of Jews as monsters are dropped as a matter of fact. And hatred of minorities is infectious: now we are seeing a genocide directed towards Christians in the Middle East and they are fleeing the region of their religion's birth.

In some ways the moral case for an exclusively Jewish state is the Holocaust. Civilised, educated Germany and anti-Semitic governments in Eastern Europe utterly failed their Jewish citizens. Unfortunately it was not Europe that paid the price of these atrocities but Palestinians, who were displaced to make room for this Jewish state. Now, however, Jewish ethical identity is under threat. The fifty year occupation of Palestinian territory and building of settlements on their land is in breach of international law. With 500,000 Jewish settlers illegally living in the West Bank we now see the children of Holocaust victims become occupiers and colonisers. We know that many of these settlers have emigrated from Europe and the US and are from families that have never had any traceable ancestral connection to Palestine. They are doing so at the cost of Palestinians whose families have been there for centuries.

But before being too quick to judge the Jewish state I will put up my hand up as a Christian to confess complicity. Throughout history Jews were the Christian scapegoat. Well before Jews were seen as a race by the Nazis they were seen as a religion whose old covenant had been revoked by the new covenant. The great reformer Martin Luther was initially sympathetic to Jews, as he blamed Catholic ineptitude for not preaching the Gospel effectively enough to make the Jews convert. But after his reformation, when they still did not convert, he turned murderous. He had some terribly anti-Semitic things to say. He agreed with a school of thought that the Church had superseded Israel as the people of God and inherited all of God's promises once made to the chosen people. Jews were, therefore, disobedient in not seeing this truth and refusing to convert. And of course the claim that the Jews had killed Jesus led to pogroms, expulsion and, in Lutheran Germany, to Nazi concentration camps. The complicity of the Reich's bishops, who obeyed Hitler and not the Gospel, was shocking. These German Christians even broke off ecumenical relations with the International Church, as God had a special plan under the Führer. Some Lutherans in the Confessing Church, like Dietrich Bonhoeffer, resisted both their own bishops and Hitler and lost their lives.

After the Holocaust Christians felt deeply ashamed. The Catholic Church, which also was largely silent in Germany, declared that the Jewish old covenant stood, as the gifts and calling of God are irrevocable. It accepted that Jews can benefit from the new Christian covenant without believing in Jesus. This was the Vatican's attempt to draw a line in the sand after centuries of persecution of Jews.

National myths to recover an identity

Every secular culture that denies religion too stridently seems to need to find a substitute, or else it swings back to religion's bosom. In the French Revolution, Robespierre went for an audacious substitute with his Cult of the Supreme Being. It failed. Alex de Tocqueville marvelled when visiting the US in the 1800s that religion played such a constructive role in building community; in France the Church had been too reactionary and allied to the aristocracy to be useful. The ex-KGB atheist now known as President Putin has swung back and wrapped himself in the Russian Orthodox Church. Like the modern czar that he has become, he (reputedly the richest man on earth) gifts them huge sums of state money for new churches and urges young Russians to go back to church. The Patriarch of Moscow, the leader of the Russian Orthodox Church, effectively returns the favour by telling people Putin is God's leader for the nation.

In 2013 I was asked to be a leader of the Civil 20 (C20), a group that works to represent issues facing civil society (such as inequality, poverty, climate change and women's rights) in the meetings of the G20, a forum for the twenty biggest world economies to set global financial policies and architecture. It is much more representative than the UN security council as it includes India, Brazil and Indonesia and covers 85 per cent of world trade. Thanks to this inclusivity it was able to quickly stabilise banks and trade in the 2008 global financial meltdown. As a representative of the C20 I had a conversation with Putin at the G20. Putin seemed interested that I, a reverend, was a civil society leader. His interest made me worry that I was too cynical; maybe he genuinely felt concern about the moral vacuum at the heart of Russian life and truly wanted the young to find meaning in an Orthodox faith.

So I tested my cynicism by suggesting that I knew how offended the Russian Church was by Pussy Riot singing and protesting at the Cathedral of Christ the Saviour in Moscow. But I wondered aloud why the Church hadn't offered forgiveness and overlooked the insult, rather than seeing them imprisoned and sent to Siberia. A look of befuddlement flitted across his face as if to say, 'Why would the Church ever do that?'

Now that is what I mean by civil religion. It undermines the fundamental tenets of a faith and distorts it to serve political or social purposes. Putin was determined to deal with the political threat of Pussy Riot. Any dissent had to be slapped down mercilessly. The religious offence was a pretext and secondary to this political interest of being in control and supressing dissent. Even worse, Orthodox faith was hijacked from its true message of forgiveness to further a political motivation. The Patriarch of Moscow called Putin's bombing in Syria a holy war. This failure is as much the Church's as Putin's. A genuine prophetic faith is when you have proximity to those in power, but you are not in their pockets.

Milak and the neighbours

In June 2013 I was visiting Syrian refugee camps to see World Vision's work there. It was heartbreaking to see the Bekkah Valley crammed with tents and broken people who only wanted peace and to return home. World Vision are providing shelter and child protection in what we call 'child-friendly spaces', as so many kids have no schools or education and are totally bored. Most importantly, we are the largest partner of the international community World Food Programme and, when managing food cash, saw funding cut from $30 a month per person to $13.50 a month. We immediately saw the mass exodus begin, simply because people could not feed their families. People poured out of the camps trying to get to Germany to begin a new life. There was a profound loss of hope that the war would end and a widespread belief that the international community had forgotten them.

After my visit I went for a walk to clear my head. I was reeling with the loss of hope. It was about 10 pm and I was wandering aimlessly. I heard a Lebanese voice greet me in broken English. I looked over and saw a man waving me into the front of his house for a coffee. He put out his hand and said his name was Milak. As

I entered his front garden I saw a group of six Syrian refugees sitting around a fire and sharing his coffee. I said, 'Oh, you've already got guests.'

Milak smiled and corrected me. These refugees were living with him under his roof, and he was giving them what work he could in his solar panel business. He said they had been there six months and had nowhere else to go. I knew that this was a common story, as Lebanon's population of 5 million now has 1 million Syrian refugees who cannot go back home until there is peace. I had seen tens of thousands just like them that day in the Bekkah Valley camps.

I asked Milak whether the refugees spoke English, and he said no; but he had learned it when taken in as an orphan himself and raised in Beirut by Christian nuns. I asked Milak if, as a Christian, he supported President Assad. He answered yes, but nuanced it by acknowledging Assad is a butcher; but as an Alawite (Shia minority) and with a more secular world view, Assad is more tolerant to Christians and all minorities in Syria than the Sunni rebels would be if they won. He shrugged fatalistically and said, 'So I support Assad.' I asked about the Sunni refugees he was feeding and housing; what was their political allegiance? He said, 'Oh, they get up early and pray to Allah, and I know they pray for victory for the rebels.' That set me back on my heels. With my family I know a little about political differences and sharing them under the same roof — this peaceful coexistence of Muslims and Christians under the same roof was impressive.

I quizzed Milak about how he lived with these tensions. Why had he taken them in? He paused, shrugged again, and said, 'Because they are human and they are vulnerable.' I sipped my coffee and then a thunderbolt hit me. Was this not the meaning of an old story originally told by Jesus a few kilometres south of Beirut some 2000 years ago? A man was going from Jerusalem to Jericho and fell among thieves, who beat him, stripped him, robbed him of everything and left him for dead. In that story it was not his own mob of co-religionists who helped him — they passed on by — but a person from a different tribe and different religion.

In that story there was a detail that Milak helped me to see afresh. The thieves had stripped the man naked. That meant those who passed this beaten up Jew could not tell from any clothing markers if he was religiously or ethnically one of theirs. Likewise, the Samaritan could not tell either. We know ethics seem simpler, stronger and clearer when it comes to one of our mob. Yet we are told the Samaritan, who had no clues as to who the man was, responded compassionately. I now understood why. He saw a human who was vulnerable. Milak was this Good Samaritan. Milak was transcending tribal ethics to include the stranger and reliving this ancient story.

After thanking him for his signature Arab hospitality to me, a total stranger, I did not wander back to my bed so aimlessly. My faith in humanity had been renewed and I had a resolved determination to be like that Lebanese Samaritan called Milak. Thank God for such random meetings.

A rule-based
international order

By 2015 the Syrian war had been raging for over four years. Tens of thousands of children had died. None of us working in the relief effort could pierce the hard hearts in the rich West. We told stories and showed terrible pictures of children suffering, but it moved so few. People simply would not give to the desperate plight of those who had fled or were displaced in Syria.

But then Alan Kurdi, a three-year-old Kurdish refugee, drowned, his body washed up on a Turkish beach. The image flew around the world and suddenly donations started pouring in. It changed Australian government resettlement policies as the government reluctantly announced it would take an extra 12,000 Syrian refugees in response to community grief at that image. What had changed? People had seen a little boy floating face down, alone, and dressed like one of our kids. He was no longer just a stranger. The Turkish policeman carrying Alan's limp body in his arms reminded the collective subconscious in our culture of the pietà: Mary, the mother of Jesus, bearing his limp corpse.

We all know that human rights are universal and indivisible. But none of us get out of bed for abstract principles of justice and rights. It is people who touch us, and it is their particular stories that take universal concepts from our heads to our hearts. This is the challenge of abstract human rights. They need a spirituality and connection that speak to our souls so we recognise ourselves in others' suffering.

Human rights in principle were intended to roll back national rights. Human rights assert that nations have limits on the rules they can make, the morality they create and their right to claim blind obedience from their citizens. Universal human rights transcend the authority of the nation state and each state promises to observe and implement such universal human rights — that all humans are born free and equal in dignity and rights. In principle no one country grants these rights and no one can take them away. So what is the authority that does grant these rights? The language is an appeal to a 'spirit of brotherhood: humanity'. Here is a spiritual authority dressed only in spiritual power that echoes a spiritual truth.

Of course war crimes, discrimination and persecution mock these human rights and nation states remain sovereign and above international law, with no effective international power able to punish their crimes. Sadly those tribunals that do exist, like the International Criminal Court, can only reach and arraign human rights abusers in weaker nations by forcing them to hand over their national criminals. Just one civil war in one nation, Syria, demonstrates how abuses of human rights by a president can engulf the world with its troubles.

It is one reason my spirituality needs to believe in a future judgement. It allows me to cope with injustice here, to forgive and not give up because I believe that this life is not the final word of judgement. Other traditions have an equally beautiful spirituality. The Dalai Lama was asked the question, 'Why didn't you fight back against the Chinese?' He responded with a smile, in a gentle voice: 'Well, war is obsolete, you know.' Then after a few moments, his face now serious, he said, 'Of course the mind can rationalise fighting back ... but the heart, the heart would never understand. Then you would be divided in yourself, the heart and the mind, and the war would be inside you.'

We are all in this together

In an increasingly global world, with the free movement of money, ideas and trade, I suspect we will eventually see the logic of the free movement of people prevail. Birds and animals do not recognise national boundaries, and even the morality of boundaries is suspect. We are all migrants as we all came originally from somewhere in Africa. Even Indigenous Australians came from there, taking generations and 2000 years to walk. In their case, 50,000 years here in Australia is an unusually strong claim! But so many more recent claims to original homelands, to a manifest destiny and a god-given exclusivity, are suspect. Often political conservatives who emphasise strong national boundaries are the same ones who oppose climate change measures. Of course, unhindered climate change will only send more environmental refugees our way, and the same conservatives cut overseas aid that would assist people to get out of poverty and stay in their homeland.

Our mental image of the nation state as an unassailable ocean liner just pushing away a few desperate people in boats has to change. The world is now one giant ocean liner, sailing on troubled seas. We are all in this ship together and can no longer just bat away the desperate. Nor can we build walls high enough, turn back enough boats and control or militarise all boundaries. In a global village we need a global imagination based on a deeper organic spirituality.

This mentality is resisted by the nation state, but it's important to remember that only 200 years ago there was hardly an entity called the nation state. Borders and passports were meaningless. So would we not be better to anticipate a future world where we return to that? Let's start by being more open at the edges — at least incrementally — today. No one country can accept the 60 million refugees on the world's books. But together we can come up with some solutions. As conservative politician and deputy to former Chancellor Helmut Kohl, Heiner Geissler, said, 'Europe has 500 million people and we are facing integrating 1 million. If you were at a party with 500 guests and one more turned up unexpectedly would anyone say, "Sorry, there's no room for one more"?'

So let richer nations accept that, say, 1 per cent of our population each year will arrive as economic and political refugees. Let's anticipate what is coming and phase this into our plans and be ready for the future. Let's educate and train our refugees and absorb them into our values, which is exactly how multicultural secular nations built themselves to become so prosperous.

Here in Australia, with an annual immigration quota of 150,000, we could stop cherry-picking only skilled people from the developing world. Why not make refugees fifty per cent of our annual migration, which on present figures would lift our refugee intake from under

20,000 to 75,000 a year? We could then encourage other nations to follow our example and end refugee camps. I have visited camps like Dadaab, in the Kenyan desert, that has been there for 25 years with over 350,000 people waiting and losing hope! A fortress mentality cannot work in the long run so why not be proactive?

If we think the refugee crisis ends when the Syrian War is finally settled, think again. The youth demographic time bomb in many African nations sees so many without opportunity, and they will be headed to the West in such numbers that Syrian refugee numbers will look minuscule. And yet nations like Australia have cut all aid to Africa as if giving them hope to stay and have a future there is simply not our problem. This is so short-sighted.

Desperation and distance

We can all accept our ethical responsibility for a fellow Australian. Their need and distress is an immediate tug on our heartstrings. But we shirk that ethical tug when it is a stranger who arrives on our shores. They are not our responsibility.

What upsets me is that we know a regional solution is the only way. The Malaysia Solution under the Gillard government was our best hope for obviating the people smugglers' business model, but it was shot down by Tony Abbott in opposition.

Australians have been paralysed for fifteen years in the ugliest debate of my lifetime. Of course, it's about refugees and asylum seekers who come by boat — we are not as hysterical about Europeans who flew here and overstayed their visas; we don't call them illegals. It is boats full of persecuted and poor people that worry us. And yet almost all our forebears came here as convicts or economic refugees on boats.

The current government came to power on a promise to stop the boats and the tragic drownings that happen when the boats are dangerous and overcrowded. I agree that the people smugglers needed to be stopped in order to save lives. But I think the Rudd government decision, taken up by the conservatives, to exile even genuine refugees forever on Manus Island in Papua New Guinea was disproportionately cruel. I sensed how heavy-handed this policy is when watching a BBC panel in mid 2015 about the crisis of those fleeing Libya and drowning in the Mediterranean. The host asked whether Europe should embrace the Australian solution of turning back the boats. Each panellist replied something to the effect of, 'No, because we are not barbarians.'

Well, bigger walls, militarised borders and turning back boats may work for a short time. But it is maintaining aid levels to give hope to Syrian people in the refugee camps in neighbouring countries that is essential. Even Chancellor Angela Merkel cut aid levels in 2014. Yes, she later courageously told Germans to welcome these 1 million refugees, but was this foolish when the refugees had no legal means to get to Europe and had to spend their savings on people smugglers to do so? Better to maintain aid and contract out German jobs to these refugees in the camps of Jordan and Lebanon. When people have hope that they can work and provide for their families then they are much more likely to wait for the war to end so they can go back home. That is what they want to do. Sadly, after remarkable patience in waiting, so many Syrians have seen the war enter a fifth year and have lost hope. What is there to return to? And without education for their children and enough to survive on in the camps, who can condemn them?

I am amazed at how casually we rationalise our approach. We love the argument in Australia that we are one of only three nations with an on-shore refugee resettlement program from the camps. We tell ourselves we are already generous because we take a few of those refugees who wait in the queue. But consider how quick we are to support the argument that the refugees cannot genuinely be persecuted or in fear as many arriving here have already reached a safe country like Indonesia or Malaysia, where they are not being persecuted.

Our geography at the bottom of the world gives us a leave pass to judge their motivations. It is not for us to share the burdens of those with unlucky geography like Kenya, Jordan, Lebanon, Turkey, Pakistan, Indonesia and Malaysia — those countries near the conflict zones that take in most of the world's millions of refugees.

And how does it sit with our conscience to have funded and built camps in nations like Manus Island in Papua New Guinea and Nauru, outsourcing our responsibility? We pay for the security forces patrolling the camps, but should anything adverse happen it's the responsibility of the local government, not us. Asylum seekers, even if when processed and found to be legitimate refugees, must stay in those nations or go home because we have decided that anyone who attempts to come here illegally by boat can never settle here. Our justification is that this approach at least stops the boats and some drowning. The cynicism of this arrangement is compounded by the fact that the countries hosting our deported in their camps are the only countries who did not suffer any Australian aid cuts; we need their complicity to solve our challenges.

These camps are not run to standards Australians would find acceptable. Yet when charities working in such places as Nauru blow the whistle, saying that children are suffering and guards trade cigarettes or longer showers for sexual favours, the charity is expelled.

We had a Royal Commission into institutional child abuse in Australia, rightly interrogating the practices of offending churches and schools and saying 'never again'. Yet we are doing it again. We are doing it institutionally under our asylum program. I believe we allow it because they are only strangers.

Beyond our shores

I well remember the first disaster I was sent to by World Vision — it was in Darfur, Sudan in 2004. I was so overwhelmed by the war, brutality and systematic rape of so many women in the huge refugee camps that I collapsed in tears at the large press conference held when I returned to Melbourne. The surreal civility of home set me off when describing the evil I had seen.

But despite my best efforts, we failed to raise much money. The human brain seems wired to only deeply respond to innocent suffering through natural disaster. Suffering due to war does not excite us or prompt generosity because we think, 'Well, they should just stop fighting.' But the suffering inflicted by war is just as real.

I was reminded of this when I spoke about Australia slashing its overseas aid program to the lowest level in our history. I was on television comparing how another conservative prime minister, in the UK, had done the exact opposite and maintained the UK's contribution at the level all rich nations have promised to the world's poor: 70 cents for every hundred dollars of the gross national income. In my view this was a lifesaving promise; you do not break promises to those whose lives are dangling by a thread. Australia, which is much richer per head than the UK, with much lower public debt, had just cut its aid level down from 34 cents to 22 cents for every hundred dollars. Prime Minister Cameron had resisted similar measures, saying, 'We will not balance the books on the backs of the poorest.' That was courageous leadership and a demonstration of true conservative values. I was making the point that we in Australia had become a nation of shirkers. Shirking our share of the international responsibility for the nearly 1 billion who go to sleep hungry each night, and shirking promises that we as a rich nation had signed up for. Of course, I received a barrage of tweets — mostly angry ones, saying something to the effect of 'why should we look after anyone else; we should look after our own'.

But the debate was suddenly cut short by the plight of Pistol and Boo. Johnny Depp had flown into Queensland to film the next *Pirates of the Caribbean* film, bringing his family and his two terriers, Pistol and Boo. Because they'd arrived on a private plane they'd avoided our customs rules and Depp's dogs slipped quarantine. At the same time as I was arguing for increased aid, our agriculture minister, now the deputy prime minister, went ballistic, saying, 'I don't care whether or not he has been twice voted the sexiest man in the world, he can bugger off and get those dogs back to California within forty-eight hours or I will have them euthanised.' Well, the uproar that followed dwarfed the Twitter outrage that I had been subjected to. Within an hour there was an online petition from thousands of Aussies demanding that Johnny's dogs be spared, and the media could hardly have been more frenzied if a president had been murdered. Any concern for refugees or African lives now at risk due to Australia's cutting 70 per cent of its aid there, or for poor Asian countries where there was a 60 per cent cut in our programs, evaporated. No, the news of the night was the fate of Boo and Pistol.

We are often more wired to help animals than humans because they are innocent — particularly puppies! But all suffering is suffering. William Wilberforce, who tirelessly fought indifference to slavery and helped to abolish the slave trade, also helped establish the RSPCA, fighting against animal cruelty. His Christian faith did not discriminate between human and animal suffering.

Outcasts and solidarity

The Rohingas are Muslim people, originally from Bengal, so they are the scapegoats in predominantly Buddhist Myanmar. They are also persecuted in Bangladesh. But the Buddhist Burmese government, including some Buddhist monks, has acted the most atrociously. In a nation with ongoing wars between many of its tribal groups and the central government, the one thing that seems to unite the Burmese is hatred of the Rohingas. The aim is to force them out.

They suffer terrible discrimination. Unlike any other minority group, they are denied Burmese citizenship even though they were brought there by the British from Bangladesh over a hundred years ago. As they are not citizens, their assets can be seized. They alone are the subject of laws about how many children they can have. Attacks by Buddhist monks and other citizens triggered a mass flight of Rohingas. They packed into thousands of tiny boats, but were turned away by the navies of neighbouring nations. Forty days later the world finally woke up to a story that thousands had been at sea for over a month and they were dying.

How is this possible? Because for the first time, Burma's neighbours, Thailand, Indonesia and Malaysia, who have housed hundreds of thousands of Muslim refugees in huge crowded camps over the years, seemed to be against the Rohingas too. They picked up a technique straight out of the Australian playbook: turn those boats back and do not let them land.

It was first used by Prime Minister John Howard in 2001 towards boat people rescued by a Norwegian ship called the *Tampa*. Although in Australian waters, the captain was not allowed to land these desperate people here. This harsh approach was so hugely popular it brought Howard back from certain defeat to a stunning election victory. His famous words, that 'we will decide who comes to this country and when' may have hurt our international reputation but it worked electorally. Both sides of politics saw this as the new electoral holy grail. If in trouble, play the xenophobia card! Simply put, fear and racism towards outcasts works as an electoral strategy (although we never openly admit that's what it is). So the Rohingas, fourteen years later, are the latest victims of this determination to play marine ping-pong with people's lives.

It's particularly nonsensical of us to demand the Rohingas' boats be turned back. Turn back to exactly where? The Rohingas are stateless. No one would accept them.

But then a few fishermen in Aceh shamed their own government and us and rescued and housed some Rohingas against their own government's wishes.

These same Acehnese, who suffered shockingly in the tsunami of 2004 and received global support, became the Good Samaritans — apparently the only ones left in our region. This international scandal ended, thanks to their bravery, and their actions prompted a change of heart. Malaysia, Indonesia and Thailand let the Rohingas land, on the condition that other nations assist in resettling them in new countries. The US, the Philippines and others put their hands up. But when our prime minister at the time was asked if we would take any, he said, 'Nope, nope, nope.'

Yes, there are 'economic' refugees among them, and yes the lasting solution is diplomatic. It is to get Myanmar to change its pernicious policies, and to get the economic refugees in Bangladesh to see a future worth staying for there. With the election of Aung San Suu Kyi there is more hope. But we do not have much credit in our diplomatic account. Why would Myanmar listen to us after we 'turned back' refugees to countries with far greater numbers of refugees than us? Who are we to lecture them to change their policies of discrimination? What moral or diplomatic leverage do we have after cutting our aid to their poor by 40 per cent? One of our poorest neighbours, and this is our show of solidarity. What a sorry mess.

Back in the 1970s at the end of the Vietnam War, hundreds of thousands of Indo-chinese people took to boats to flee the expected Communist reprisals. Neighbouring nations closed their borders and left them to die at sea. World Vision was outraged and

International President Stanley Mooneyham bought a Panamanian ship, calling the operation 'Sea Sweep', and started picking up dehydrated and dying refugees. The ship kept trying to dock at Hong Kong, Singapore and Malaysia to offload its passengers, and was turned back by these governments. No nation wanted to help.

With time running out World Vision ran an international advocacy campaign and shamed these governments, including that of Australia, about their hardness of heart. Prime Minister of Australia Malcolm Fraser was particularly touched and Australia was one of the first governments to respond and agree to resettle these Indo-chinese refugees if the neighbouring nations allowed them to land. The US and Canada soon followed. Australia has never looked back from the boon of taking in these desperate refugees who became upstanding Aussie citizens. A glorious chapter in our recent history.

PART III

From violence to forgiveness: Love your enemy

Christian faith and violence

My journey with faith has also meant facing faithlessness as I engage in the flux and fears of life. This is particularly so when I reflect on the issue of violence. I must remember that the good news of Jesus conquered the mighty Roman Empire. Loving their enemies, praying for their persecutors and caring for the poor wherever they found them, Christians turned the empire upside down in a few hundred years.

Rome did not have a welfare system. By 250 CE, the Christian community in Rome was supporting more than 1500 destitute people daily. Throughout the empire, churches were running the hospitals and schools and providing the only welfare safety net for the poor, whatever their religion. Jesus' teaching, that the 'last shall be first' and the 'least the greatest', unleashed a social force that panicked Emperor Julian (331–363 CE). He became fearful that Christianity might take over the empire by stealth of good works. So he wrote to his priests, insisting that their temples to Roman gods throughout the empire should introduce a welfare system like the one in Christian churches. Prison visitation, hospitals, orphanages and poverty relief were commanded by imperial edict. He donated massively from his own coffers to kick it off. His letter to Arcacius in Galatia, dated in 362 CE, confessed: 'It is disgraceful that … the impious Galileans support not only their own poor but ours as well, all men see that our people lack aid from us.' But Emperor Julian's program failed, because if your spirituality and your gods do not support loving the unlovely, your charitable efforts will ring hollow.

Today, many who say they follow the vision of Jesus actually in practice are very disconnected. I was surprised when, in the Margaret Thatcher lecture in 2015, Tony Abbott, a former Australian prime minister known for his strong Catholic beliefs, lectured Britain that they were being badly led astray by what he described as the 'wholesome sentiments of the Good Samaritan' in opening up to refugees trying to enter the UK. Now, you may agree with his political advice and geopolitical instincts. But for any devout Christian who believes in the vision of Jesus, this was hard to hear! In truth, the former prime minister was showing loyalty to the nation-state and its fixed boundaries by recommending repelling refugees in desperate suffering, not loyalty to Jesus.

It would have been more honest for him to be transparent and nuance his argument by saying that Jesus' teaching had much wisdom, but was not equipped to handle public policy or face today's refugee challenges. Margaret Thatcher herself famously did this by saying once that the whole point of the Good

Samaritan story was that he had money in his pocket and was in a position to financially help the desperate man on the Jericho road. Her moral was that nations need to be prosperous and have their finances in order if they want to help! I think the real point of the story was seeing the image of God in another, even if there were no religious or ethnic ties, and a positive duty to assist — but that's just my personal interpretation.

On the debit side of the ledger, the Christian triumph in capturing the Roman Empire proved a pyrrhic victory. I have discovered in life that it is not your failures that prove to be your greatest danger but rather your successes, and so it proved for the Christian faith. With the conversion of Emperor Constantine, Christianity was declared the state religion. This nonviolent movement became the military enforcer. Christians whose nonviolent Messiah had been crucified by this empire became Christian soldiers bearing a shield with a cross. The greatest champion of the powerless became the chaplain of imperial power, gaining titles and Church tax exemptions and privileges along the way. Christianity became a diluted faith, shaped into the cultural–political glue for uniting the empire. (After the collapse of the Roman Empire its seductive prototype was revived by the Holy Roman Empire, which ruled with force and heresy trials and repression.)

The marriage of church and state under Emperor Constantine meant Roman Christians now did not have to choose between loyalties, but it shattered the alternative spirituality of Jesus, who resisted the false peace of the empire to announce God's partiality for the poor and humble. Success had blinded the heart and Christian triumphalism was born. It is still playing out, though thankfully with much dissent from disciples throughout history who have practised the original spirituality. In many isolated pockets Christians have always stayed true to the power of this original transformative vision.

If you are wondering how the spirituality of 'love your enemies' lent itself to the slaughtering in Christ's name of the Crusades, Christian triumphalism is the answer. For the first 300 years of Christianity, Jesus' followers refused to serve in the military. With Constantine's conversion, they moved from pacifism to being soldiers fighting under the imperial insignia of the cross. Later theologians tried to justify violence by teaching a just war theory. It was meant to support the right to defend yourself, but the theory was extended to justify Christian imperial wars. The problem was always the adjective 'just'; and self-interest too easily rationalised 'justice' as our side going to war.

I lean towards pacifism, although I am not an absolute pacifist as I cannot imagine every situation. But I do believe war has outlived its usefulness and rarely achieves the goals we intend, and using religion as a political tool for military purpose is always wrong. We are currently living with the painful blowback of this approach.

I was first personally exposed to religious violence while I was at the seminary in Switzerland: the stories of our Nigerian colleagues who had suffered from Muslim–Christian tension, the Israeli bombing of Lebanon in 1982 and the massacre of thousands of Palestinian women and children in the Sabra and Shatila camps. My fellow student and dear friend Zahi Nassir, an Arab Israeli from Nazareth, was humble and accustomed to suffering but it was seeing his tears for those Palestinian refugees that brought home how this conflict was so personal. How could I go to a theology class with him and ignore the reason for those tears? It made me realise that the Bible was not limited to being a book for my personal guidance, but could be turned to in asking the big issues of ethics in the public square.

I did my thesis on John Howard Yoder, a Christian pacifist theologian. He taught nonviolent resistance. In essence, his argument boiled down to this: Christians cannot follow Christ and ever practise violence. We are not God and so cannot destroy the image of God in another — even if they are an enemy. Tolstoy also had some pointed questions: he asked why the Church never suggested that Jesus' condemnation of adultery needed to be reinterpreted, while thoroughly reinterpreting his stance against war and violence. For his trouble, Tolstoy was excommunicated by the Russian Orthodox Church.

In those Cold War days while I was a student, with the real prospect of a nuclear war looming over us, we asked how many deaths could be justified in defending our freedom and our way of life. Among my student colleagues were Swiss and Spanish citizens who had refused compulsory military service because they took

Jesus seriously, and they had suffered imprisonment as a result. I admired their faith: they refused to hand over their conscience to a military superior who might order them to kill someone who had done them no harm. They had a subversive spirituality that believed in nonviolent resistance, and took the consequences.

Faith's shadow

I was taught the piano as a child and one of the many hymns I learned to play was called 'The Old Rugged Cross'. It has a haunting melody. The lyrics spoke to me about a love that did not know when to stop — a love that went right over the top even unto death on a lonely rough cross that was 'the emblem of suffering and shame'.

As a child growing up in the 1960s I had seen many disturbing pictures of Ku Klux Klansmen in their pointed hats and ghostly white robes, and their ritual climax in the burning of a massive cross. I knew racism was wrong, so it came as a terrible shock to me when I first heard that the prelude to the lighting of the giant cross was always the crowd singing 'The Old Rugged Cross'. These Christians regarded desegregation laws as a transgression of the Bible. They saw Lyndon B. Johnson, who legislated the *Civil Rights Act* and enforced desegregation in schools and public facilities, as Satan. I have never again been able to sing that dear hymn without shuddering because of this shadow. I have come to understand that distorted faith can feed a human desire to feel superior; so many of us are intent on justifying why we are better than others. All I can plead is that the most important teaching of the New Testament is that all have sinned and all have fallen short of God's standards — all. None are better, none are inferior, and none can save themselves without the help of God and the support of a circle of love. These are the sentiments of 'The Old Rugged Cross'.

As a Baptist, I was shocked to read Reinhold Niebuhr's words that if a drunken orgy was going on in the American South then you could be pretty confident there was no Baptist participating — but if a lynching of a black man was proceeding, you could be sure there would be Baptists participating. Any pride in my religious mob evaporated. They had asserted their superiority in the most brutal, unchristian way.

Even today the image of faith is literally black when we think of it in relation to ISIS: black burqas, black flags, black propaganda and black deeds like crucifixions and beheadings. Martyrdom through terror and the fetishisation of death by suicide bombers while perpetrating evil on innocents, both Muslim and non-Muslim, is a religious impulse. To deny that is foolish. The call for a Caliphate may be a political act, but it comes from a religious motivation to restore the pure eighth-century rule along the lines taught in the Qur'an. We are all fed up with this expression of faith and how it is hijacked for political purposes.

Jonathan Sacks describes this as altruistic evil. Everyone knows that it is evil to kill and rape innocents, yet ISIS boasts about it on YouTube. (Even the Nazis had enough shame to try and hide their murder of innocents.) But in the ISIS world view, their actions are altruistic and for the greater good of us all; they're building a better world that is submitted to Allah, ruled by sharia law, where women will be protected and all will flourish. Of course, those outside their faith do not agree, but in their minds it is a better world.

Underlying this behaviour is a clear spiritual need: to overcome shame or humiliation by imposing death. Shame is negativity turned inwards; humiliation projects its energy outwards. It is a problem most religions try to address. Some, like Buddhism, advise detachment, viewing shame and humiliation as an illusion. Christianity recommends repentance, forgiveness and grace. In Judaism, violence is born from shame and humiliation: God is pleased with Abel's grain offering, but rejects his brother Cain's meat sacrifice. Cain is humiliated and murders his brother Abel. James Gilligan, a psychiatrist who has worked on death row in US penitentiaries, says that his clinical experience has taught him that most of the vicious murders all proceeded from the same emotion: humiliation. A murderous rage turned outwards.

Other religions offer atonement, sacrifices and scapegoats to deal with shame and humiliation, and in this sense scientific Nazism functioned in some religious ways. The humiliation of Germany by the Versailles Treaty saw Hitler blame a scapegoat — the Jews — who had to be sacrificed. Other religions address it via ancestral offerings to restore disrupted harmony in one's life.

Since the fall of the Ottoman Empire and the carving up of the new national boundaries from Iraq to Syria and Lebanon by Christian nations after World War I, Arab politics has been riddled with humiliation. All post-Ottoman Arab political parties were formed after the humiliating end of the Caliphate and against a backdrop of colonial humiliation. This humiliation at the dominance of the Christian West has been a theme for Arab Islamic nations, whether secular or theocratic. The planting of a new Caliphate flag that ignores those insulting Western-drawn boundaries, like Syria and Iraq, is a remedy for that humiliation.

It explains the puzzle of how so many Western Muslims who previously were merely cultural Muslims, often with a history of drugs and partying, can suddenly find religion and purpose in Islamism, which satisfies their sense of humiliation and rage with the trappings of piety. There is an important distinction here between Islamism and Islam. Islamism is the attempt to impose Islam on others, whether through political, revolutionary or violent jihadist means. Islam, on the other hand, like most religions, is remarkably diverse and is neither for peace nor war; its main purpose as a religion is to address the human heart.

Sunnis make up 85 per cent of Muslims worldwide, but we need to remember that only two strains of Sunni Islam regard other Muslims (Sufi, Shia) as heretics who need to renounce their beliefs or die. Equally they see Westerners as infidels who deserve political subjection or death. These two strains are Salafism, which originally sought to reconcile Islam with modernism, and Wahhabism, which rejected modern influences. Both soon shared a rejection of traditional and scholarly interpretations, opting instead for a direct fundamentalist reinterpretation of Islam. Not even all members of these two groups accept the logic of violent jihad as the only expression of their beliefs. Certainly most Sunnis do not subscribe to this hardline version made visible by Al-Qaeda, Boko Haram, the Taliban and ISIS.

Most of the bombers who perpetrated 9/11 came from a town in Saudi Arabia. Their town was affluent, and they had any number of creature comforts, as well as great career options. Why did they feel the need to commit such atrocities? While it could be justified by a faithful interpretation of the Qur'an — that infidels in the US forces stationed in Saudi Arabia were polluting and desecrating the holy soil — it can't be the only explanation. I believe their belief in paradise fused with Sunni Saudi public humiliation at US occupation of their holy land and anger at their own monarchy and its rulers. In Islam's invitation to jihad these men found the religious gifts of atonement for shame. In violent deaths they longed for transcendence, community and significance by giving their lives to serve Allah and submit to his will. These are the fundamental things that we all long for and, when twisted and repackaged up in political religion, they can be lethal.

Recently I spoke at an interfaith gathering of Muslims, Hindus, Jews and Christians in a church in Melbourne. The speaker after me was a Muslim woman wearing a hijab. She told the excruciating story of her best friend, whose husband slit her throat when she told him she was unhappy and thinking of leaving him. The speaker recounted her grief and she directly related this horrible act of violence to her Islamic religion and its treatment of women. She said, 'I am loyal but my religion is in deep trouble because we have taken two essential things out: women and spirituality.' She spoke of growing up in Syria where in Damascus she learned the Qur'an and Ahadith at the feet of female scholars who sat with the men and were treated as equals. She mourned how this had changed, with men claiming all the power of teaching and interpretation. Repression of women justified by religious interpretation had shocked her. Spirituality was at the heart of Islamic belief and this had been replaced with fear and force. For herself personally, she kept faith that Islam is indeed a religion of peace by focusing on spirituality.

Religious faith can be used to justify truly horrific actions, whereas true spirituality is always unequivocally pro life and pro respect. Remember the attack on a school in Peshawar, Pakistan, where members of the Taliban murdered 145 people, 132 of whom were children? When asked how they could do this, a Taliban supporter, as quoted in *Islam and the Future of Tolerance* by Sam Harris and Maajid Nawaz, said:

Death is not the end of life. It is the beginning of existence in a world much more beautiful than this ... Paradise is for those of pure hearts. All children have pure hearts. They have not sinned yet ... they have not

*been corrupted by their unbelieving parents. We did not
end their lives. We gave them new ones in Paradise,
where they will be loved more than you can imagine.
The last words they heard were Allahu Akbar. If your
faith is pure you will not mourn them, but celebrate
their birth into Paradise.*

This is perhaps the purest expression of altruistic evil I
have read.

Scapegoating religion

The issue for all religions, particularly Islam at the moment, is to reject violence. Religious scholars are still struggling to insist on an unequivocal condemnation of violence in the name of God or faith. This is a struggle because it feels like one must show disloyalty or infidelity to sacred writings (the 'revealed truth' from God), many of which explicitly call for violence. Many religions cannot resolve the violent bits of Scripture that are problematic and often directly contradict those same Scriptures' messages of love and neighbourliness. Even the great soul Mahatma Gandhi squibbed this one. Ambedkar, the lower-caste drafter of India's constitution in 1948, pleaded with Gandhi to abolish caste and its institutionalised religious violence. Gandhi refused because as a Hindu he thought it would irreparably damage Hinduism.

But it is equally the issue for atheists or secular ideologies. Until the French Revolution in 1789 every community, state or empire in human history was religious. Fewer are officially religious today, but lots of terrible things are still done by leaders in the name of God. Even after the French Revolution and the advent of secular government and separation of church and state (a very good development), what a dismal story of brutality and violence still. Empire, nationalism and colonial acquisition were at the heart of World War I, in which 10 million people died. Nationalism and race drove World War II, and 60 million died. Ideology for a universal proletariat drove the secular Soviet Union, and 20 million died under Stalin. Many died under Mao and the cultural revolution. Pol Pot imposed a communist ideology and a million Cambodians died.

Secular ideologies and secular nationalism are littered with corpses. The problem, then, is not religion or secularism, but human fear and aggression to the 'other', whatever its political dress.

As a religious person I am committed to dealing with the issue of violence in my faith, and never sugar-coat that complicity. But it is time to face up to our human condition and stop scapegoating religion.

The problems of interpretation

Unbelievably, ISIS does not regard many of its Sunni co-religionists in Saudi Arabia as faithful enough to the Prophet. Apparently there aren't enough beheadings and amputations for adultery by the Saudis. The 'true' Muslims' cry is always for greater fidelity to Sharia law, to purity and to all the teachings of the Qur'an and the glories of the Umayyad Caliphate in the seventh century.

Sharia law is mainly, but not totally, spiritual. It is praying five times a day, travelling to Mecca once in your lifetime, confessing there is no God but Allah, and giving alms to the Muslim community. There is no conflict with any of that to our secular rule of law. But for some true believers, Sharia includes the total legal package covering what we call criminal and civil law. While some are absolutely dedicated to restoring a seventh-century understanding of those criminal codes, I believe the great majority of Muslims do not buy into this. But I sympathise with their dilemma. If you are not calling for utter fidelity to your religious texts, are you cherry-picking and compromising what seems to be clear in the full Qur'an or Bible?

I don't believe so. While the scriptures themselves may be timeless and unchangeable, our *interpretations* of those texts are not timeless and infallible. A study of any scripture shows that interpretations differ among scholars and in different contexts and historical times. There is a plurality of interpretations, and no one is indisputable. Pluralism logically follows, and pluralism demands that condemning others as heretics because they have a different interpretation is unfaithful to the god you worship. You are acknowledging fallibility in *interpretation*, not in the Scriptures, and this requires tolerance of your co-religionists' perspectives — not judging their faithfulness or orthodoxy.

This is the reformation struggle already underway in Islam between what we who are outside the faith like to describe as moderates and conservatives.

How many animals, and humans have to die?

There is another archetypal dimension to civil religion. It is the ritual sacrifice of the innocent through war. The shedding of blood atones, forgives and sees a resurrection of a sort after a massive defeat — in this case of a nation. We see this not just in the best-known example of Jesus' sacrifice, but also in history and in other religions.

Ancient Romans were remarkably tolerant towards many minority religions. They did not enforce worship of Roman gods and did not persecute Christians or any other religion for not subscribing to Roman gods. But there was one thing that was non-negotiable. As the gods kept order in heaven, this was mirrored on earth; so, for there to be order and peace on earth (the Pax Romana), they required all faiths to sacrifice just once a year to Roman gods. Many paid this low entry ticket for political peace, and some Christians paid their pagan neighbours to do it on their behalf to buy peace. But the majority of Christians had a firm belief that the sacrifice of Jesus had satisfied God once and for all, granted humans forgiveness, and that order under the reign of God was established. In one sense their cry was 'enough blood and no more animal sacrifice'. This was the offence for which they paid dearly.

In rage at this political snub, the Christians' refusal to maintain the Roman gods who granted stability to the empire, successive caesars ordered that the Christians be dragged to the Colosseum to their deaths. Christians were prepared to die because they believed that more innocent blood did not need to be spilled to get to God and be accepted by him. That the true God was not dangerous, demanding and distant. They reversed the logic of a primal religion that believed in a God whose distaste for us could only be overpowered with human or animal sacrifices or self-flagellation. The reversal was stunning. Instead of spilling more blood to get to God, we had God in Jesus spilling his blood to get to us and show us his love. God was saying, 'Enough of this. It is settled.'

For Australia, many assume our national identity was born in the sacrifice made by the ANZACs. This most prosperous, blessed and advanced of nations where no blood had ever 'stained the wattle' in a struggle for independence still yearned for a blood sacrifice in order to truly gain its self-respect as a nation.

For Americans, their fight for a more perfect Union or no Union at all was the Civil War. The economics of slavery were so profitable that it is unlikely it would have ever ended as an institution without a war. But the bloodshed of brother against brother and South against North that cost over 600,000 lives was a horrible price. The archetypal overtones were picked up by President Lincoln as he tried to make sense of the senseless in his second inaugural speech. He asserted that, if American slavery is one of the offences against God:

> *fervently do we pray, that this mighty scourge of war may speedily pass away … Yet, if God wills that it continues until all the wealth piled by the bondsman's two hundred and fifty years of unrequited toil shall be sunk, and until every drop of blood drawn with the lash shall be paid by another drawn sword, as was said three thousand years ago, so still it must be said 'the judgements of the Lord are true and righteous altogether'.*

Can we ever transcend this need for blood sacrifice?

Love your enemy

Dealing with violence has been a theme of so much of my later ministry and work. We have made huge strides in defeating global poverty, but not in conflict zones and violent fragile states like the Congo, Somalia, Afghanistan, Pakistan, Syria and South Sudan. When I started at World Vision in 2004, 30,000 children under the age of five died every day from stupid poverty. Stupid because we have enough food and we know how to create clean water and we have medicines to treat preventable disease. Today it is less than 16,000 children who die each day. We now know how to eradicate absolute poverty in stable poor nations. But with poverty retreating into conflict zones, our progress is blocked.

I once thought that violence was neutral. If deployed to take out bad people, then it is good, even redemptive — but if violence is deployed to take out good people, then it is bad. This was not Christian thinking, which taught that good and bad run through every human heart, including mine, and so violence can never be redemptive.

Yet this thinking of redemptively killing enemies had infected my faith — as it has Islam and secular powers that have decided their enemies must be liquidated. As I studied the Bible with a lens on these public issues, I added some more rings to the tree of my faith. I discovered that Jesus was more than a personal saviour who rescues me from a sinful world. He invited me to participate in the mission of bringing God's rule on earth, which was justice and peace. Jesus taught that the reign of God would displace the powerful and elevate the least to being the greatest and the last to first place. The meek would inherit the earth.

World Vision is working in Afghanistan, Pakistan, Northern Iraq, Gaza and many other Muslim-majority poor nations doing relief and development. We have huge programs with Syrian refugees in Lebanon and Jordan. In fact, our footprint serving Muslims is far bigger than that of Islamic Relief or any other Muslim charity. We are often criticised for this by other Christian development agencies that choose only to work through the Church and focus on the world's Christian poor. They ask if we've swapped sides. I readily remind them that Jesus never told us to only love Christians or suggested Christians are superior.

This 'in group' bias undermines true faith and spirituality. In a discussion on national radio with an archbishop from Sydney, I reminded listeners of Jesus' criteria for salvation: whether we had fed him when he was hungry, clothed him when he was naked, invited him in when he was a stranger and looked after him when he was sick, and that 'when you have done this to the least of these my brothers you did it to me'. The

Archbishop took exception and said the 'least of these my brothers' refers to Christians and is not a general ethic beyond Christians. This is 'in group' bias.

Actually, Jesus went much further and told us to love our enemies and do good to those who persecute us. He had this novel idea that even your enemy is made in the image of God, and so love and turning the other cheek can transform them from enemy to a friend. As Martin Luther King Jr put it in his book *Strength to Love*:

> *love is the only force capable of transforming an enemy into a friend. We never get rid of an enemy by meeting hate with hate; we get rid of an enemy by getting rid of enmity. By its very nature hate … tears down; by its very nature, love creates and builds up. Love transforms with redemptive power.*

But the idea that everyone carries the image of God is a troubling notion, counterintuitive to our sense of loyalty to our own tribe and religion. When religion gets rolled up in nationalism and our people are fighting over there, then it is explosive to give support — even if it is aid to Muslims in poverty.

Forgiveness

Tribalism in its darkest deepest genocidal fury was experienced in Rwanda in 1994. In just eight weeks, a million people, mainly but not exclusively Tutsis, died by the machetes and rifles wielded by Hutus.

In the 1930s Belgian colonialists had ordered the registration of Tutsi and Hutu, largely creating a differentiation that made little cultural sense. It meant nothing in practical terms; both groups spoke the same language, KaRwanda, many had been intermarried, and all were largely Christian.

But after this 'administrative registration' the Belgians and the French played divide and conquer games, driving a wedge between Hutu and Tutsi to bolster their own colonial power and economic interests. The French have still never apologised for their culpability. When the killing started the UN withdrew its peacekeepers and Bill Clinton refused to act. This is one reason why he continues to return to Rwanda and to apologise repeatedly that it was the worst mistake he made as president.

I returned to Rwanda in 2014 for the twentieth anniversary of the genocide, as World Vision has played a major role in the reconciliation process. I would never have believed the depth of reconciliation in so many lives unless I had seen it with my own eyes. It has given me hope. How do you deal with so many offenders in a nation that is broken? The unspeakable atrocities were followed by a local form of justice known as *Gacaca*: literally, grass courts. The surviving elders formed courts under trees and in villages and encouraged murderers to confess and reveal how loved ones died, where the bodies were buried. For their confession they would receive some discount on prison years. Many went to prison, and twenty years on you still see chain gangs of prisoners in yellow vests.

While the law is the only tool we have to make people equal, it can never restore wrongs completely. How can justice ever really be satisfied? It is only ever partially realised in punishment. This is where the reconciliation process comes in. The idea was simple: they realised they had no future as a nation if they could not forgive. They realised they'd go on living half-lives, crippled with resentment if bitterness was allowed to rule. And if they lived like this it might all erupt again!

Much of the process proceeded down lines familiar to our thinking. Cooperate and confess, serve a shorter sentence and be released to start again. But a Christian faith insight became central in order for many to draw a line in the sand and to courageously move on. It was that forgiveness needs to be offered even before repentance. Mercy needs to be shown first, as it assists people to then confess. If there is such an assurance that they will not continue forever as a despised murderer even after serving their time, then we can all be healed. The phrase I heard from so many survivors whose loved ones had died in shocking circumstances was 'I had to forgive first' so the offender could know they could confess and have a chance to be reintegrated. The faith insight is from the New Testament: while we were still sinners, Christ died for us. Before repentance, love and acceptance were extended.

I have not witnessed grace like this too often.

Rwanda is now known as the Switzerland of Africa. Its roads, infrastructure and education are all superior. It is a phoenix rising from the ashes, and the progress in twenty years has been phenomenal. Brokenness has moved to wholeness.

Sometimes forgiveness has to be offered even where there is little prospect of reconciliation. In Jerusalem, Ardeer is an Armenian Palestinian. She and her family lived in the Armenian convent in the Old City of Jerusalem's Armenian quarter. She has one parent who is Catholic and one Orthodox. Jerusalem is a religious Disneyland and multiple identities are normal. But as a Palestinian watching the loss of liberty and space for her ancient community, she hungers for normalcy and the freedom to have a coffee in a nice place. But she is boxed in and prohibited from visiting the places of her childhood. I asked her how she felt about the occupation, and she took a deep breath and said, 'I choose not to be bitter. I forgive the Israelis who have taken control of my life and diminished my freedom.' Her personal forgiveness has little prospect of bringing reconciliation, but it is still right.

The same was true of Dr Jack Sara, president of Bethlehem Bible College. He grew up in the old city at the seventh station of the cross, on the Via Dolorosa. He was a young man full of rage and he went to prison twice in the Intifada for throwing stones at Israeli military vehicles. A huge percentage of Palestinian youth have been in prison! But then he experienced a life-changing conversion and became a follower of the Palestinian Jew: Jesus. He knew he had to forgive and stop living in a fog of bitterness. But that has not made him blind to the injustices his people suffer. At the Bible College he pulled back the curtains in a classroom to show us Palestinian roofs. We saw water tanks on every roof. Even though the water aquifers are in the West Bank (where Bethlehem is), because of the occupation Israel takes most of the water and Palestinians are reduced to catching their water in roof tanks. Often there is no water. But Jack goes on forgiving and believes in the way of nonviolence.

The story Jack, Ardeer and I seek to indwell is not an empirical formula for success. But it not only gives meaning; it gives a faith resource to live differently. It does not make us passive: we know that you must try and *be* the message, not just a preacher of that message! Both of them are heroes for me as they live in the mess and muddle and remain faithful to a higher vision: to love. They epitomise the message of Jesus, who called even on the poor and oppressed to repent and love their enemies. Why? Otherwise, without such repentance, the underdogs, if they got power, would just oppress their former tormenters and the cycle of violence would continue. The heart needs changing, not just the structure.

PART IV

Convictions for
the world

Economic morality

Frankly I am perplexed that so many seem to think that economic growth through more individual incentives is the answer to the issues of the global commons — particularly when much of that growth uses fossil fuels that are choking the planet. Even the G20's infrastructure and economic growth agenda begrudgingly admitted it must be 'inclusive growth' — that is, inclusive of the environment and inclusive of the poor. After all, what good is economic growth that just continues to flow to the top 1 per cent? The more unequal a nation is the more prisons and security forces it has, and the worse physical and mental health outcomes it experiences. Inequality is now recognised by economists as the major blockage to sustainable economic growth. It is good for no one, ultimately, even the rich. But the seductive story that says 'the richer I am as an individual the happier I will be' remains.

It is certainly true that the greater wealth a *poor* person has, the happier they will be. If you cannot guarantee your children enough calories to survive or clean water or an education you feel the panic of failing them. That is real unhappiness. But we also know that, at a certain income level where our needs are met, we cross a threshold where greater wealth means greater stress and less time for community and relationships. We are caught in a race that has no real end and, though we loathe admitting it, we have lost the purpose and meaning of why we are running.

The father of laissez-faire capitalism, Adam Smith, tried to address the meaning issue in his book *The Wealth of Nations*. He said by harnessing the individual's self-interest we do good for everyone. His most famous line: 'We do not owe the beer we drink or meat and bread we eat to the benevolence of the brewer, butcher or baker but to their self-interest.' But he had a much bigger purpose than economic theory and applauding the self-interest of individuals; he was a moral philosopher first and foremost and wrote about it in his *Theory of Moral Sentiments*. His fundamental question was how society holds together, given that so few people are virtuous. He wanted to explain why people behave irrationally, given it was rational to obtain material necessities and then to cease striving and working for more. It is only, he wrote, in the 'imagination' that the supposed 'pleasures of wealth and greatness' become 'grand and beautiful and noble' and their attainment 'well worth all the toil and anxiety which we are so apt to bestow upon it'. But for him all this striving for riches and honour was delusional behaviour and a sign that few people attain virtue. Nevertheless, this irrational behaviour promotes the common good because this 'deception … rouses and keeps in continual motion the industry of mankind'.

Even the 'proud and unfeeling landlord' who does not care at all about the poor but only 'the immensity of his selfish desires' can actually consume 'no more of the harvest than that of the meanest peasant' and that means he will have to spend some of his surplus on luxury and thereby ensure that poor receive 'a share of the necessaries of life, which they would in vain have expected from his humanity or his justice'.

So his economic insight was that self-interest coordinated by markets fulfilled a deeper purpose — human community and promoting human sympathy — resulting in a compassionate justice that was lacking in our character. His invisible hand was not the market, but Providence or the Author of Nature who anticipates and then uses greed for the common good. Such Providence aims at solidarity and the inclusion of the poor. Mysteriously for an economist, Adam Smith believed that God/Providence does not exalt greed but enlists all these millions of self-interested market choices by irrationally driven individuals and, through his invisible hand, weaves a greater good and justice. I suspect most prefer his economics to his theology, but he was crystal clear on what he believed to be the deeper purpose for markets: to create justice. His understanding of the free market could not be further from the neoliberal economic rationalists of today.

Smith was acutely aware that human compassion does not extend much beyond a person's immediate circle. He even gave the example of a man's response to news of a great earthquake in China: humans will profess compassion and concern before going to sleep 'to snore with the most profound security over the ruin of a hundred million of his brethren'.

Yet times have now changed in a way that Adam Smith did not predict. We are now an utterly interdependent global village. Our world is now a global waterbed: every compression somewhere in the world pushes up serious troubles for others in a different place. From global epidemics such as bird or swine flu or Ebola to the interlinked global banking systems to climate change and terrorism, neither individualism and self-interest nor national self-interest is an adequate response in the global village. All our problems are now global and no one nation can pull the right levers to fix them. We need a global ethic and global governance to respond to global issues.

Solidarity with creation

As Albert Einstein said, 'The most beautiful and profound emotion that we can feel is a sense of mystery. This is where the meaning of all art lies, all science. The man who is no longer familiar with the sense of mystery, who has lost the ability to be amazed and humbled when faced with the creation, is like a dead man or a blind man at least.'

Primarily it is my faith that drives me to want to address the challenges of suffering and big issues like climate change. I am not a scientist, but when I see what the science says and then experience in our development work how so many poor farmers from Africa and Asia are now only getting one crop a year where for millennia farmers got two, something has clearly profoundly changed. I want to act, partly out of Christian compassion for them, but it's rooted in my faith that the 'earth is the Lord's' and we are its stewards, not owners. The arrogance of ownership too often leads to unsustainable practices that may maximise profits but defy the Creator and ultimate owner. My faith teaches that creation and its biodiversity also carries the image of God, not just humans. It too was created and so deserves sacred respect.

The failure to address climate change affects both the faith-filled and the unbelieving with threat of a creeping environmental apocalypse. I believe it can only be resolved by a renewed spiritual sensitivity and reordered relationship to nature that is no longer just rationalist. The main antagonists in the fight (denialists and climate change activists) do not seem to understand that objectification, scientific debate and technological fixes are not working. Neither do they have a language for the spiritual challenge.

On one side appear scientists and secularists who think it is just a matter of presenting the evidence. NASA tells us that the hottest ten years in human history have occurred since 2000. In Australia they say our temperature has now conclusively risen 1 degree over the last hundred years — equivalent to pushing us 150 kilometres closer to the equator and explaining bushfires, droughts and the loss of crop production. Weather volatility in extreme rains, cyclones and droughts is a near universal experience. But facts without spirituality just seem to bounce off us.

On the other side are the doubters who are happy to proceed on an argumentative factual basis. In the overreach of scientists presenting 'indisputable evidence' of climate change, these doubters only need to raise a reasonable doubt, which is not difficult. Look at how the tobacco industry survived untouched for decades: they did not need to show that cigarettes were safe but just cast doubt on the findings that they were so dangerous.

Spirituality is about heart and intuition, not just head and facts. It is about the mystery of relationship and deeper organic connections. As a Christian who explores spirituality within that tradition I use the word 'creation', not 'nature', as it implies a relationship with the Creator. It suggests that we are seamlessly connected in a spiritual union and our future or fate is collective. A relationship can only succeed based on humility and respect along with giving and receiving. A Creator for me suggests that all species, not just humans, carry the image of God and that, rather than assume humans can just dominate nature by clearing forests and losing species by burning fossil fuels for economic gains, we rediscover that the earth is not ours but the Lord's.

My spirituality is based on following one who always refused to accept the dualistic boundaries of in and out, righteous and sinner, material and spiritual, master and slave, male and female. One who flouted the purity rules to go to the outcast and servant. Environmentally he spoke of foxes that have holes and birds that have nests but he owned no roof under which to lay his head. He spoke of a relationship with the transcendent.

Taxation is the cornerstone of order and democracy

I t was Constantine who first exempted the Church from paying tax because they cared for the poor. This was the first recognition under Roman law of the provision of a social safety net and the Church had defined itself as non-discriminatory in its inclusion of the poor. Despite Christians doing a disproportionate share of the heavy lifting in Australia (twenty-two of the twenty-five biggest charities in Australia are Christian faith–based) there are repeated public calls from secularists to remove their tax deductibility. Unlike in the US, churches here do not get a tax deduction on the donations they receive. They get no state tax exemption for their religious purposes.

We know that taxation has existed for at least 2500 years because it is described in Mesopotamian writings. It started without money: the first form of taxation was paid in goods in kind, including paying with your labour. We know levies were imposed on imports and exports, and there is a Babylonian record of a person being imprisoned in 1990 BCE for smuggling, which demonstrates that tax evasion is pretty old. In the Old Testament there were personal levies (a poll tax) and taxes on land. But there was a fairness instinct: in the Book of 2 Kings it is said that tax should only be taken from 'the men of substance' and that King Jehoiakim 'exacted the silver and gold from the people of the land proportionately'. Capacity to pay and what we call progressive taxation have been in play forever!

When we consent to paying our tax it is no longer our money. The refrain 'it's my money' is used by the rich to justify their evasion in tax havens. Yes, there must be debate and accountability over government spending. Our opportunity to review our consent to tax and spending is at an election but, until then, assuming proper appropriation and budgets, it is not our money. In fact the main instrument of social justice in a nation is a progressive tax as it expresses solidarity with the poor. And the rich have no right to complain; their wealth did not materialise solely from their own cleverness or hard work. They all enjoyed education and infrastructure such as roads, hospitals and police to prosper. That is social solidarity and should not be undermined. As the great jurist Oliver Wendell Holmes Jr on the US Supreme Court said, 'I like paying tax. It is the price I pay for civilisation.'

In April 2016 we learned the dirty little secrets of the rich and powerful thanks to the leak of 11 million emails from the Panamanian legal firm Mossack Fonseca. Dictators, democratically elected politicians, so many wealthy individuals and corporations have been robbing us blind. Some $32 trillion in wealth is stashed offshore in tax havens by wealthy individuals alone (trillions more by corporations) to evade paying their tax, leaving the bills for hospitals, schools and infrastructure to us tax-paying suckers. Governments have been robbed of billions in tax revenue for education and hospitals every year this dirty little secret persists. We've always suspected that for the rich paying tax was optional, but now we know it! A light has shone in dark places and exposed the unreasonableness of the global market and its rules.

World leaders and 128 politicians, film and sports celebrities and some 800 wealthy Australians are named in the files, along with twenty-five billionaires from the *Forbes* Rich List. These people are robbing their national jurisdictions of tax using some of the 214,000 shelf companies set up by this law firm. Their stashes sit alongside those of drug dealers, criminals and arms salesmen. These wealthy non-taxpayers had all relied on these shelf companies and secret arrangements being kept secret — until the leak. Now we know that the elite 1 per cent hide their money offshore and dare to use it to corrupt our democracy!

And even governments are totally hypocritical. The stash of cash does not stay in Panama or the British Virgin Islands in shelf companies, but flows to the banks in the financial centres of London, New York and Sydney in the guise of investments that politicians laud as achievements that their policies attracted.

What is righteous?

I was intrigued when I read a book called *The Righteous Mind*. It asked why good people are divided by politics and religion. In it the author, Jonathan Haidt, suggests that conservatives and progressives actually have emotional differences built into their psychological makeup. He believes that we have gut responses to issues like fairness and no amount of reasoning will change these. Indeed, reason is only used to vindicate and justify the gut response we already have, but otherwise rarely changes our minds. Both groups share two moral foundations that are organised in advance of any experience.

The first of these is a care/harm foundation that developed in response to caring for vulnerable children. It makes us sensitive to signs of suffering and need and to despise cruelty to the helpless. The second is the fairness/cheating axis. But then the two groups diverge. He suggests that, while progressives mainly value these two foundations, there are some more moral foundations that are more the domain of conservatives: loyalty/betrayal, authority/subversion and sanctity/degradation.

There are fascinating experiments he cites to arrive at this observation. He gave this scenario to progressives and conservatives: A woman who lives alone finds an old American flag and cuts it up to use it as a cleaning rag. Has she done something wrong? Progressives would shrug and say, 'No, not really.' But conservatives would say, 'Of course she has.' When asked why, conservatives would say it's because the woman would feel guilty doing that to the flag. They would try any argument to justify their outrage, and nothing would shift their conviction that she had done something very wrong because the loyalty/betrayal axis is so strong in conservatives.

This difference in relevant moral foundations was made clear to me at a meeting held in 2014 before the G20. The Australian prime minister, Tony Abbott, graciously met with a delegation from our Civil 20 (C20) group after our Civil Society Summit and before the G20. At this Civil Society Summit we formulated our recommendations and were officially passing them over to him, as president of the G20 meeting in Brisbane. In our delegation there was a representative from Russia, Turkey, China, the US, Britain and myself as the chair for Australian Civil Society. As C20 delegates we presented Tony with our recommendations on climate change, tax havens and multinational tax avoidance and inequality. Our gut was squarely located in the fairness/cheating sphere.

I noticed Tony's eyes glaze over. When he responded, he wanted to talk about ISIS. To be fair, he had just come from a media conference about terror and so it was uppermost in his mind. But he had begun that theme with me in the lift on the way to the meeting, and continued it in front of the international delegates. He responded to their climate change concerns by pointing out how lucky we were to even be able to raise those issues; we wouldn't if we were under ISIS. He even returned to the issue as we went down in the lift at the end of the meeting and parted ways. We at the C20 do not minimise terror, but it was not on our agenda. But Abbott's gut was in the harm/care, authority/subversion sphere, so it was hardly a meeting of minds.

Shared-power stories and public office

In my search for meaning I am fascinated that my gut responses to many issues are often so different from those even of members of my family. Where does that come from when we share the same gene pool and the environment we grew up in was so similar? (In our family the main things we discussed were religion and politics: the two things most families steer away from to avoid trouble.) Of most interest to me is how the same religious beliefs have led to different political beliefs. Where did our paths diverge and why?

Christians often say to me that if only there were more Christians in Parliament then we could sort out all our problems. Secular people, on the other hand, point out the disproportionate number of active Christians in Federal Parliament. They are right; it is hugely disproportionate to the general church-attending population.

Once upon a time, budding Australian politicians were warned not to talk about their faith, as the public would take them for religious nutters. Faith was to be kept private and was seen as a political handicap, unlike in the US, where it is de rigueur to talk about God and his blessing on America.

My how things have changed. Prime Minister Kevin Rudd was a prominent God-botherer, and he pioneered an Australian Labor Party caucus of God-botherers as he pointed out that Labor had needlessly alienated the church vote. His faith certainly convinced him of the need to increase wealthy Australia's commitment to the world's poor. His global vision is broad and correctly sees the nations of the world as all occupying berths on the one ocean liner.

But it was not just Rudd. Deputy Labor leader Tanya Plibersek asked me if she could speak (about aid cuts) at a gathering World Vision conducted for a hundred Church leaders. She spoke passionately and, when she was asked how we could pray for her, she said, 'Pray that my heart will not become hardened to the needs in our world.' Good answer. When a conservative Christian senator heard she had spoken at this gathering, as it was reported in the religious press, he was furious that she got this platform as it was 'their constituency'. I replied that we are no one's constituency and regularly have conservative politicians speak — and I hope we remain free to include all and question all.

I think many people share my curiosity about how faith shapes values and public policy. A secular approach should mean no view is given automatic weight. But I much prefer the freedom to discuss why our leaders feel strongly about certain issues, and so religious disclosure is something I applaud. I have observed that conservatives tend to gravitate to private morality texts in the Scriptures, and progressives to the justice texts.

Why and how they weight these different texts is an important public discussion.

This curious mix of conservative faith and conservative values is puzzling to those of us who watch US elections. Religious conservatives take pride in the slogan 'vote your values'. Their values are pro-life, pro-guns, pro–death penalty, anti–gay marriage and anti–universal health care in Obama's *Affordable Care Act*. Are not those values a little contradictory? Particularly when so many evangelical leaders who 'vote their values' were in a rush to support Donald Trump, a potty-mouthed, twice-divorced casino-owning mogul who has clear problems respecting women, Mexicans and the disabled? The only consistent value was excessive nationalism in his slogan 'Let's make America Great Again'.

We have variants of this puzzle in Australia. Many had a problem with former Australian prime minister Tony Abbot's Catholic faith influencing his position on gay marriage, abortion, euthanasia, the morning-after pill and stem cell research. I say we all have values — far better to be transparent about the source so voters can make an informed decision.

A tale of two Tories

I know former Australian prime minister Tony Abbott's religious world and I know him because I have met him many times; my brother was a member of the same cabinet under John Howard's leadership. I have always found him a decent person with a reasoned faith. But when the first tranche of aid cuts came through I was deeply distressed at the looming prospect of ringing World Vision national directors around the world and telling them that the World Vision program that was going to protect Syrian children in the refugee camps was going to be cut due to loss of government funding. Those 6000 war-affected kids in South Sudan that we were going to educate — gone. So I wanted to talk to him and took the liberty of making a phone call.

This particular call was before Australia had made definitive these massive cuts in aid, which would crash us to the lowest level ever in our history. But we saw it coming. I lobbied Tony Abbott about the lives that would be lost and the suffering imposed. He listened courteously but responded: 'Tim, aid is only for good times and we are in bad times.'

I assumed that David Cameron was Abbott's conservative soul mate, so they would be largely on the same page. So I reminded him that Britain had increased aid and kept their promises to the world's poor, despite their government debt being 85 per cent of the gross national income, versus ours being only 15 per cent. I pointed out that Cameron's government were having to slash and burn their domestic spending in a tough economic downturn and were facing a hostile public that always wants aid cut; yet he had stood firm and remained principled. I reminded him of David Cameron's words, 'We will not balance the books on the backs of the poorest'.

I pointed out to Tony that this was a natural conservative position that he should follow. This did not go down well with Mr Abbott. He said, 'Don't talk to me about David Cameron because he did something very foolish. He cut defence — defence, Tim. You never cut the red coats. Not the red coats.' It startled me and I needed a moment to remember who the red coats were. Needless to say, he had graciously taken my call and given me a hearing but he had little sympathy and did not agree. And the results are now plain. Australia, the third-richest nation on earth, slipping down to nineteenth on the OECD table of aid generosity even as the target of 70 cents per 100 dollars of gross national income (GNI) goes down to 22 cents. The cost of one coffee every five months!

As other nations have increased aid and global aid levels have gone up for the last three years, we have cut and cut in every one of the last three federal budgets. Treasurer Scott Morrison, a committed Christian, talked in his maiden speech about his faith as his primary motivation and he explicitly related it to why he had gone into politics: to make poverty history and particularly to save the 6500 preventable daily deaths of African children. He cited as his inspiration William Wilberforce and Desmond Tutu and quoted Bono on aid to Africa. Scott Morrison has sat in a cabinet that effectively cut all Australian aid to Africa. And when he became treasurer he cut aid again! Yet this is the main national and global tool to address climate change, poverty and refugees, particularly the next expected explosion of poor refugees from Africa.

I have puzzled at this difference between two Tory leaders. I have puzzled because aid does not and should not belong to the political left or right. Our promises to the world's poor are longstanding and made by both sides of politics. And, curiously, aid was at its highest in Australia under a conservative prime minister, Bob Menzies, and cut most (before these latest cuts) by an Australian Labor Party prime minister, Bob Hawke. Generally, the rich world has agreed, whatever side of politics they are on, with the plan first formulated in 1967 by Canadian foreign minister Lester Pearson. Those nations who are blessed and represented in the OECD would give 1 per cent of their GNI, whatever their economic circumstances. Governments would contribute 0.7 per cent, and their private citizens out of their private pockets and through aid charities would contribute the other 0.3 per cent. So this is not a matter of conservative hostility to a natural Australian Labor Party agenda.

And as a percentage (not a set dollar amount) it is transparent and fair, because in bad economic times a nation with a decreasing or smaller GNI will be giving less in actual dollars. It is flexible and easily incorporated into the ebb and flow of a nation's economic fortunes without needing to be politicised. The UK is now at 0.7 per cent and has legislated this. Certainly bipartisanship has helped Cameron, as both Labour and the Liberal Democrats were on the same page as the Conservatives. Tony Blair, Gordon Brown and Nick Clegg have all been committed like David Cameron. So when confronted by hard times and a growing debt and amidst popular calls to raid aid and look after themselves, bipartisanship has seen them stand firm. This bipartisanship saw calm answers to hostile questions from the public about the level of aid when the debt was so high in the last UK election. Ed Miliband, under public fire, calmly hosed down resentment and said, 'Labour will protect health, education and aid. We have made that clear and so we will just need to take a bit longer to pay off the debt.'

Australia had a bipartisan agreement to reach not 0.7 per cent but 0.5 per cent by 2016. That would take us to giving about $12 billion a year, not the current $3.8 billion. The Labor government's fetish was focused on reaching a budget surplus, and technically they started the breach in bipartisanship as they kept pushing the annual timetable out beyond 2016. But aid was still bipartisan before the last election. When the promise was to be trashed after the election, the Abbott government suggested it was Labor's fault, as they had diverted some $700 million of the then $5.2 billion program to refugee programs. But there is simply no moral equivalence between that $700 million (technically allowed to be called aid) and the $11.5 billion slashed over the next four years by the Abbott government. That is a lot of lives and hope lost. It is now frozen at $3.8 billion, with no CPI increases. It takes us down 0.22 per cent of GNI.

But back to my tale of two Tories. Why the difference? One is principle. Both Tony Abbott and David Cameron believe in the principle of national security and spending on defence — but one turned it into a priority at the cost of development. Both believe in the principle of generosity from those who are better off to lift those in dire poverty. Yes Australia still gives aid. But Cameron was principled about balancing security and generosity and keeping the sacred promises made to the world's poor. Abbott's team, conversely, in an effort to undermine the credibility and importance of aid, ran around in opposition suggesting aid was wasted, even though an aid review headed by a former conservative colleague, Senator Margaret Reid, had found it was well directed and suffered far less fraud and waste than most domestic government departments, like those administering Australia's unemployment benefits. But prejudice seems to always trump facts, and waste and fraud was an easy message to sell to a public wanting to believe the worst about aid even though it was all untrue. I may be naive, but there are principled politicians on both sides. A believer would simply never sink so low as to trash principle even if his electoral survival was on the line.

A second difference is perspective. Under the last few governments Australians have lost perspective and have been told they are victims and they are suffering. Not surprisingly, we have become grumpy, fearful and mean. That is what happens when you turn inwards and focus only on your own troubles. But I blame our politicians more than our citizens for this mood disorder. And although this has happened under both major parties, it became an art form when Abbott was opposition leader. In his view, everything was terrible and we had a budget emergency and a debt and deficit disaster. If you listened to the rhetoric and the catastrophising you would be forgiven for thinking our situation was as perilous as that of Greece!

We have some real poverty in this nation, but I cannot tell you how much it sticks in my craw to hear Australians who live in McMansions and have two cars being told by our politicians how much they are hurting. And these people are the big voting bloc, not single mums and the unemployed. Look, Tony Abbott told the middle class, your electricity bills and petrol expenses are rising and I know your pain and I will lower your taxes and fix it — all with no cuts to health, education or the Australian Broadcasting Corporation.

Maybe the most egregious example from the Labor side of this loss of perspective came from a minister in the Gillard government who wanted to scare his own government away from raising taxes on people earning above $250,000 a year. He said, 'I know a lot of people on $250,000 a year who are really battling.' Really? If you are on $250,000 a year, you are in the top 1 per cent of income earners in the nation. How are you a battler on that? We know that people only compare up and never down, so I guess if you are on that income and meet Gina Reinhart, worth $20 billion, it may feel like you are battling.

But after meeting Gina you did not suddenly get poorer. Nothing actually changed; you are still in the top 1 per cent of income earners When I hear some Australians complaining about how tough life has become I want to shake them and invite them to come and visit the world that I see, where a billion people are trying to survive on $1.50 a day. Many do not make it. Now that would give you some perspective about the importance of keeping our promises to the poor. It would make you determined to remind yourself and your friends that we have our troubles but by comparison we are blessed. Children often get this much better as they have not been confused by politicians and comparing up. I find them refreshingly concerned when they hear about kids in poverty their own age. They know that is not fair and they want to do something.

The power of transparency

When I was a theology student in the early 1980s I remember standing at the doors of the Wittenberg Church in then Communist East Germany where in 1517 Martin Luther had nailed his ninety-five theses and started the Reformation. It was the beginning of what became one of the most far-reaching intellectual and spiritual revolutions in human history. A new awareness spread throughout Europe that the individual was acceptable to God through faith, not through the Church's control and obeying its rules. It was a cry to let God be God and not have the Church play God. It was fuelled by conscience and individual readings of the Bible, now that Gutenberg's invention of the printing press made that possible.

Luther's first thesis began with 'When our Lord said Repent he willed the entire life of believers to be one of repentance'. His second thesis was that this word, 'repentance', cannot be understood as referring to the sacrament of penance as administered by the clergy and Church.

In saying this, he was actually addressing what we know today as corruption. The Reformation was a protest against corruption. Repentance in Luther's day required penance: fasting or giving to the poor. It was left to the priests to determine what was acceptable penance. But if you died having confessed your sins but had not performed penance, then you were in deep trouble. You could not go to heaven but would have to wait in purgatory as the debt you had incurred had not been paid with acts of penance. And boy, were people terrified of purgatory — a favourite subject for the preachers of fear. It was all agony and you would do anything you could to meet the debt and help get your loved one out.

So a novel scheme was concocted by the Church. You could use a short cut and purchase an indulgence and pay the debt. Those who sold these indulgences were licensed by the Church to hear confessions of the sins of the living and speed up the forgiveness with a quick and easy payment. They could also receive a proxy confession on behalf of a deceased relative and administer absolution, springing them from the horrors of purgatory. This was a brilliant money-making scheme as the Church alone had the franchise on salvation and could sell it or even subcontract it out for the right fee.

In 1515 a special indulgence was put up for sale in Germany to raise funds so a cash-strapped Pope Leo X could complete the construction of St Peter's Basilica in Rome. So the Archbishop of Mainz, who himself borrowed to purchase his bishopric, was now in charge of the subcontracted indulgence franchise. Half the proceeds went back to his creditors and the rest to Rome. It is why thesis twenty-seven of the ninety-five that Luther nailed up said, 'They preach only human doctrines who say that as soon as the money clinks in the chest the soul jockeys for eternal rest and fly out of purgatory'. Luther, still as a faithful Augustinian monk, believed that, if only the pope knew all this, he would want to reform this abuse. Thesis fifty said, 'Christians are to be taught that if the Pope knew the exactions of the indulgence preachers, he would rather that the basilica of St Peter were burned to ashes than be built up with the skin, flesh and bones of his sheep'.

But the rottenness went right up to the top. Indeed this systemic corruption had started there. As this dawned on Luther he started to rebuke the Holy Father for going about in such a worldly and ostentatious style that neither king nor emperor could equal. This kind of splendour was offensive to his spirit and the Gospel.

I feel his rage. I have attended the UN general assembly in New York and I have seen the opulence of leaders from poor countries, who book whole penthouse suites in the most expensive hotels for a huge retinue of courtiers while their people suffer. I watched the pomp and parade of power of these heads of state from chronically poor nations living like medieval potentates. And I know that many of these same leaders have their ill-gotten wealth offshore in tax havens and Western banks.

Maybe it was why I could no longer be silent. In 2015 we gathered in Lilongwe, the capital of Malawi, with politicians from countries such as Kenya and Malawi. The occasion was a reception to explain the groundbreaking work of Tony Rinuado's Farmer Managed Natural Regeneration in re-greening Africa. We were there to talk about this magnificent program to feed and re-generate Africa, but I put environment and small farmers aside as something just bubbled up inside me. I departed from my prepared speech because I felt anger at injustice rising in me and irrationally felt compelled to protest, whatever the danger. I have learned in my journey of listening to the Spirit to not ignore this, as to do so is to quench my faith and spirituality.

So I launched forth. I told the audience that my brother was in federal politics in Australia for twenty years, but he did not go in as a rich man and he most certainly did not leave as a rich man. Now, many politicians do make good money after a life in politics, but many do not. But no Australia politician initially goes into politics in order to become rich. They go in for public service, whatever their political ideology. Then I paused, dropped my voice, and said, 'Let me be honest, as a friend of Africa, and tell you what troubles me deeply about your national politics. What worries me is that the very reason so many choose to go into politics is the motivation to get rich.'

My staff looked aghast! I knew they were secretly hoping our World Vision driver outside had the car engine running as we might have needed a quick, inglorious escape! But before we could change the subject one of the Kenyan politicians said, 'I totally agree with you. It is the curse of our system. Kenyan politicians are the only ones in the world who do not even pay tax!' What deeply impressed me was that this was Raymond Moi, the son of Kenya's second president who is still fighting corruption charges from his time in office twenty years before. It took courage for him to say, and his brother is a likely candidate for the next presidential election.

The conversation turned to why this was. I learned something about the cultural pressures on them. People expect their political leaders to be rich and own a big house and to dig into their pockets and help them. They want a successful 'big man' because that increases the honour they feel vicariously as a member of the same tribe and increases the clan's chance of support. It was a frank conversation, but I still thought, 'Well, those justifications could have been rolled out by a pope and archbishop in Luther's day.'

We too easily forget that much of today's religious participation is driven by a heart hunger that wants to expose power and corruption. Religion is a great place to organise: what other groups meet weekly and listen to sermons reflecting on the world and what is wrong in God's eyes? What other group hears stirring weekly messages to stand up for God and others and to speak out against things that are unfair? Secondly, it is often the only political space to organise against corrupt regimes and dictators. This is why the Catholic Church was at the forefront of the Solidarnosc resistance in totalitarian Communist Poland that unashamedly elevated the party comrades with elite lifestyles compared to the proletariat they supposedly represented. A Polish Catholic Pope was timely too.

Spirituality, when organised, is revolutionary. There was only an iron fist behind the iron curtain, and my travels there, particularly visiting my friends in East Germany between 1981 and 1984, gave me no reason to believe anything could challenge that fear and repression. I was wrong. In the late 1980s the Protestant Church in East Germany's symbol was a candle that they lit at the church altar every Monday before pouring out onto the streets in Leipzig and East Berlin and Dresden to march with signs around their necks reading 'Every Monday, without violence'. Soon this small, brave group of Christians was joined by tens of thousands, at first saying softly and then louder: 'We are the people.' The protests were deeply felt but always free of violence and in 1989 the Berlin wall fell.

It is very similar in the Arab world. In January 2011 the Arab uprising began in Tunis and the first presidential head to roll was the corrupt President Zine El Abidine Ben Ali, who had been running a kleptocratic state for twenty-five years. Within weeks Egyptians were pouring into Cairo's Tahrir Square demanding that General Mubarak go.

The US and the West had ignored the abuse and corruption of these Arab leaders, which is the real issue that troubles the Egyptians and indeed most oppressed populations who still hope that the democratic West is more principled. But they can discern little principle, as we have supplied weapons and aid to military dictators like Mubarak in Egypt because they were tough on religious extremism and uncompromising in fighting Al-Qaeda.

It is worth noting that we can never work out who is friend or foe. The West has backed everyone. First it was Sunni religious extremists like Osama bin Laden in Afghanistan who were fighting the Soviets and then, after 9/11, we backed tribal drug-running clans in Afghanistan against bin Laden and the Sunni Taliban who sheltered Al-Qaeda. To confuse everyone, we then supported the Shia in Iraq against the minority Sunni Iraqis and the more secular Saddam. On and on the reversals have gone; the only consistent principle is that we back those who we think act in our interests at the time. We have lost all credibility and principle and usually find we are backing the wrong horse. Why? Because we rarely name corruption as the underlying target of all these confusing shifts; but our democratic principles, which idealise transparency, should demand it.

After the uprising in Egypt President Mubarak was jailed, but the hopeful victory of people power was all too temporary. We witnessed the exuberance of Egypt's first free election after years of a corrupt and repressive military dictator, but then witnessed the shattering disappointment as the Muslim Brotherhood won that free election. Mubarak had made it impossible for the moderates in civil society to organise, and squeezed the life out of them. Only a religious community like the Sunni Brotherhood was able to organise and mobilise; it had a proven structure and machinery to win. They were ready and organised but, to be fair, although extremist, they had also done the hard yards fighting corruption — and corruption was as much the issue as freedom. So they won a democratic election. Shocked at this, we shifted again and blinked as they were overthrown in another Egyptian military coup and their election was stolen.

This story happens again and again. The religious extremists win support not because people love their version of religion, but because they are sick of the corruption and disorder. When the Afghani people saw the same warlords who had pillaged them back in power with US support, and many of the corrupt they hated in the pay of the CIA, the revulsion set in. We now suspect that President Karzai was just running a corrupt protection racket for his brother and cronies. Would we not be smarter to spend fewer dollars on terror and intelligence and more on cleaning up corruption? After all, corruption and abuse of minorities is one of the main reasons why so many of Iraq and Syria's Sunnis support ISIS. They were promised equal treatment and no tolerance of corruption. But this is now even more horribly complicated as the region explodes in a sectarian war between Sunni and Shia over the spoils of power.

But back to repentance. Repentance is a call for transparency. Because God sees all and still forgives us, we are set free and inspired to live humbled under his grace. This form of repentance is desperately needed. Repentance is needed by leaders like Putin at the head of a charade government without real checks on its power and whose financial corruption is hurting Russia. Given its vast resources Russia should be the richest nation on earth — but it is not because of corruption and the concomitant lack of investment.

Martin Luther, like his later namesake in the American civil rights movement, believed that repentance must be lifelong. Many regard the fact that Scandinavian nations are always first on the Transparency International index as the least corrupt in the world as a legacy of their Lutheran culture. They may be very secular nations now, but Martin Luther and the dominant Lutheran Church influence has seeped into their political cultures. Repentance is the religious language that aims for personal, national and institutional transparency. Both Martins brought together justice (the opposite of corruption) and the spiritual power of faith in their understanding of the Gospel to marvellous effect. It is the reformation many are praying for in Islam.

Plato posed the question of transparency in his story of The Ring of Gyges, written nearly three millennia ago. In the fable he posed the question: if a just man wore the ring of Gyges and found he could become invisible by twisting the bezel of the ring, what would he do? Would he be any different to the unjust man who had the ring and could twist the bezel and become invisible? Plato concluded, no. He asserts that the just man would also steal from the market and go into another man's house and seduce his wife and murder whoever he liked — just like the unjust man. No man would have such iron strength of will to stick to what is right in the absence of accountability. He concluded that men know what justice is, but will only practise justice when visibility means they are unable to do wrong. The evidence he believed was clear. No man is just of his own free will, but only under compulsion. No man naturally thinks justice pays him personally better than injustice, and unfortunately he is right in thinking this if there are no limits!

But then how can we live together? Only with transparency enshrined in checks and balances. My spirituality welcomes visible checks and says there is One who always sees and I am always living in the presence of at least this One who knows all. Spirituality is believing that there is always an audience for all that I say and do — an audience of at least One.

PART V

Life and meaning

So why do I believe?

To those many people who have never had a spiritual experience and think such things are probably all an illusion, at least suspend judgement until you hear me out. When I was seventeen I had a life-changing encounter. Though it was my first it has not been my last.

I had been at youth camp in the hills surrounding Melbourne called the Dandenongs. I went for a walk at night. It was not that cold and I was rugged up anyway. Suddenly I was trembling uncontrollably. I struggled to stay on my feet. I was overwhelmed with a sense that I was in the presence of God and, even more astonishingly, that this God loved me. Experiences like this in many ways are essentially wordless experiences. I heard no voice and saw no light but I was lost in awe and saturated with love. Awe because this seemed something far greater than my mind could ever conceive or fathom. Awe at the natural beauty around me that I had seen many times before but now I felt like I had truly noticed. I have no recollection about how long this lasted but when it was over I felt a new person. I walked back to the campsite feeling as if the boundaries between the physical and spiritual had collapsed and that I had glimpsed a parallel universe. I remember feeling that the boundaries between me and others had collapsed and I was equally part of them and unified. For me the primary spiritual experience was divine love. I knew that God loved me and intuitively I understood that as a part of humanity this God loved everyone — without qualification. This experience was a significant early ring on my tree of faith.

Jewish rabbis have a belief that, in order to create life, God had to show great love and experience sacrifice to make space for the existence and being of others. God had to withdraw, even surrender something, to create life. I think the ethical challenge in my work has been, 'Will I make space for others, and at what cost or what personal sacrifice?' But it is deeper than just an ethical question. It is a question of Being. God had to relinquish exclusivity and donate existence to others if they were to know and share life. If God makes space for other beings then I must do the same. Their dignity must be deeply respected even if it offends my prejudices or is inconvenient or difficult.

David Bentley Hart comes closest to articulating my experience of the divine and he gives three reasons to believe. Firstly, being or existence. From my own first encounter with the divine as a seventeen-year-old, I have been imbued with a sense of love and purpose in a sacred cosmos. In that encounter in the Dandenongs I discovered the beauty of a transfigured natural world that I had scarcely noticed. The wonder that anything exists at all and so is a pure gift from a Giver was burned into my being in that encounter. So I have never been touched by a materialist or naturalistic concept of the universe as a closed system. A naturalist view that asserts existence came from nonexistence simply makes no sense to me. How does existence arise from nonexistence, or being from non-being? How was it possible for primal inanimate cells to 'wake up' and develop consciousness that is central to being human?

Rather, I believe that it is eternal unconditioned Being that donates its being or existence to animate all contingent, natural and living things. Existence is not a natural phenomenon and so cannot be susceptible to natural explanation. In this sense it has to be *supra* natural. It is prior to any physical cause. I find materialism's explanation of existence much more magical thinking than my faith.

Without that simultaneously transcendent and earthly spiritual being that pulses through all life, I do not know what to do with beauty, love and wonder — not to mention ethics and intentional purpose. Neither do I have any sense of Good and what it means to live a good life. I am lost. For me the question of why the solar system exists or I exist or why anything at all exists points me to Supreme Being. By this I do not mean the technical intelligent designer of the Deists — a lesser god who works with inherently lifeless and purposeless materials in creating and then retires to let the system run. That is still just the world as a machine tinkered with by a superhuman intellect. I mean by God the source of existence. As David Bentley Hart puts it,

'To see the cosmos as wholly pervaded, unified and sustained by a divine intellectual power [is] at once transcendent and immanent.' This is what the Bible names as the Logos.

I resonate with the Apostle Paul (who was himself quoting Greek philosophers) when he said, 'In Him we live and move and have our being.' Or, if you want a Hindu social activist voice, Gandhi said, 'We have no existence whatsoever outside and apart from God.'

Secondly, consciousness. In that divine encounter at seventeen I experienced a change in my consciousness. I viewed myself and the world differently. Even after we can explain every electrical impulse, chemical trigger, nerve ending and synaptic cell in the human brain, we will still not be one iota closer to explaining consciousness.

We can certainly understand which parts of the brain influence consciousness, but a mechanical view of the brain, the world's most sophisticated instrument, can never get to the internal subjective experience of the 'mind' of a person. Neither can psychology explain intentionality and the rational mind that seeks truth and beauty. I prefer to believe that the Supreme Being is also the Supreme Mind and this is why the transparency of the universe is open to consciousness and comprehensible. As a matter of science, we could not empirically discover subjective consciousness if we did not already participate in such consciousness. We can perhaps empirically still discover atoms and organisms that are not visible. But it takes a mind that is active, not one passively receiving stimuli from the physical world, and assumes a consciousness imbued with rationality and will to seek and impose categories that do not exist prior to consciousness.

I am fascinated by cultures, beliefs and people. I plunge into discussion, as only an extrovert can, wherever I am. I am fascinated by deep conversations with total strangers from different cultures when I am travelling and am always surprised. I am trying to understand their subjective interior world. This curiosity is never satiated. It expands my understanding but always leaves me admiring the mystery of consciousness and the uniqueness of the individual mind. Difference in cultures explains much, but not everything. I suspect that even after we can explain all the extraordinary events that precipitated the Big Bang, we will still not be any closer to understanding consciousness. Consciousness and its mystery point me to a conscious God or Supreme Being.

Thirdly, joy. The surprising surges of joy or exuberance in my life, and those I see in others, are amazing and inexplicable to me without God. The joy I sense at the prospect of trying to do good leads me to believe that God is good. The beauty I see in a finite object of art is not wholly contained in the object itself but exists because I have an intuition of a transcendent sense of beauty. Longing for truth, for an understanding of reality, grants me purpose and a desire to see the profound interconnectedness of the world.

I was the judge of the religious Blake Art Prize in 2016. The winner was a Hindu artist, Yardena Kurulkar.

It was titled *Kenosis* and comprised a series of fifteen photos of terracotta replicas of her own heart dissolving in panels in water. She saw it as an attempt to capture the erosion, resurrection and elusiveness of human life. It gave me joy reflecting on the fragility of the organ that pumps life through my body but also I saw the heart as the organ of love, however contingent and fragile. It caused me to reflect on absolute love that is unconditional and gives love as the purpose of life even when it is dissolving as we live. It offered perspective on why my work with the world's poor is less about 'doing' something for them and is more about 'being' with them in solidarity, friendship and inexplicable joy despite poverty and suffering.

Love is a universal grammar. Bliss or joy is not the goal of consciousness, but it is a signpost to something beyond the material here and now — transcendence. I am also being eroded and my life is often elusive but my faith gives me joy and love as it lingers. As CS Lewis said, 'Joy is the serious business of heaven.' I remember having a profound experience standing in Gaudi's La Sagrada Familia Church in Barcelona a few years ago. Gaudi was once asked, 'Does it worry you that you will never see your magnificent work finished in your lifetime?' He replied, 'My client has all the time in the world.' This timeless thinking, so different to modern thought, took my joy to a whole new level.

But you might ask why I assume God is benevolent. Is there not enough evidence of suffering in the world to suggest that the Supreme Being may be malevolent?

Some readers may even be annoyed that I seem to be too exclusively Christian in my talk about Jesus. But the reason is that my faith in benevolence is only solved by being specific. Only if I can tie the word 'God' to the story of Jesus can I make this leap of faith. If I did not then the malevolence of God would be an equally plausible interpretation of the evidence. It is not just an arbitrary decision for me to see benevolence and not malevolence, but rather a specific faith leap in this revelation of God in human history. My lived experience has upheld what I absorbed in my early years — that good can outdo evil, that hope trumps despair and simple shoots of life emerge from the worst of disasters, be they natural or human-caused.

The simple answer is that I choose to believe in benevolence. It is a leap of faith I make because I am encapsulated by a vulnerable God who has entered our world and embraced our suffering humanity — not a distant, unfeeling Being. It is why I see God in the face of Jesus.

Living meaningfully

As a result of my upbringing, my understanding of salvation is that it aims at understanding and wholeness. To be whole is to live with my faith even if it puts me at risk of suffering and scorn. My faith engages with the real world and is not an escape; it involves joy and sorrow, blessing and burden. My faith envisions a society where all have a place at the table, whatever their birth or status.

There are forms of Christian theology that see salvation as individuals booking their tickets to the great U2 concert in the sky, with faith functioning as a reservation card to book their place. This is not wholeness, but flight. This approach can also be found in other religions and in Western New Age pursuits. I admire the spiritual discipline and searching of my New Age friends, but am amazed that so many tell me not to worry about injustice or environmental concerns because it is all an illusion. Their spirituality, with its sense of unreality about what I regard as real suffering, is just another form of individualistic escape.

For me, spirituality is different from philosophy in two ways. While philosophy seeks knowledge and intellectual understanding, spirituality is more about the choice to trust. I choose to trust and, though I am utterly limited in my understanding of so many of life's imponderables, such trust leads me to try to live my life faithfully and meaningfully. Secondly, faith (unlike philosophy) has to be experienced and lived by ritual, worship, community, prayer and meditation. It must be embedded in my daily rhythms, and it must be embodied: literally felt in my body, not just my mind or spirit. And it is communal. At a communion service I walk forward with others, publicly acknowledging my brokenness, and receive in the bread and wine forgiveness.

I know that philosophical truths have a theoretical beauty in their breadth, consistency and rationality. But they are less important to me than what works in my daily experiences. Each day I try to experience beauty. Each day I try to face up to my own brokenness and face up to the evil I see in the world. And at the end of the day I try to ask: Am I more whole, free and reconciled? So I reflect on encounters, conversations, deeds and stories to see what meaning emerges. The puzzles continue, but this is my resource in living meaningfully.

My first job at the end of school in 1972 was in the cosmetics department at the Myer store in Melbourne's CBD. I have never been a style icon, and at seventeen years of age I was even less so. Unsurprisingly, cosmetics soon proved to be an incompatible fit for me. Despite my mates' sniggers and my ignorant bungles, I am grateful for the job. Working in the warehouse at the back of the store there was a very quiet, petite, diligent middle-aged woman with a heavy Eastern European accent. One day, one of the other workers discreetly pointed out a number tattooed on her arm. I did not understand the significance of it, and so he explained. I was shocked and, with all the blithe indiscretion of the young, tried to engage her in conversation. She politely rebuffed me and pulled her sleeve over her tattooed wrist.

But despite her reluctance to talk, this fleeting encounter had a huge impact on my life; it has continued to haunt me. While her sleeve could cover that tattoo, nothing could erase what had happened to her. This example of innocent suffering in the face of human evil disturbed my faith, which had taught me that, if not one sparrow falls to the ground without God knowing, then His eye is even more on humans and He will protect those who are good. But was not Jesus innocent and good? Yet he was falsely accused and executed. I can only explain innocent suffering in my faith by believing that this God also entered human history and has personally suffered. So the cross and resurrection is the answer to human evil that imposes innocent suffering. An innocent man crucified in the name of Roman racism and militarism defangs the powers of racism and militarism through his resurrection. Christian faith is not a recipe for protection and flourishing, but it does have a story to address evil.

Since then I have met many Holocaust survivors and heard their stories. One woman in St Kilda told me about her two daughters and how, in 1942, she went to hide one with neighbours who could only take one child, leaving her other child at home. She successfully hid one child, but the Nazis detained her on her way home and transported her to a camp. She never saw her other daughter again. The woman told me about her recurring dream. She is at our famous fairy penguin beach at Cowes, Victoria, where every evening visitors can view the penguins waddling ashore at sunset. In her dream she sees a baby penguin that is lost and alone and separated from the others. In her dream, no mother penguin ever arrives to protect and guide the baby to safety. The defenceless baby penguin is alone on the beach, waiting.

While I cannot fathom the depth of the emotional pain this woman experienced, I have felt a shade of this survivor guilt myself. When I come back from disasters or witnessing people in dire poverty, I feel guilty that I can board a plane and leave while they are trapped. On a few heartbreaking occasions I have turned my back on desperate mothers who have offered me their children to raise as my own so they can have a better future.

I feel guilt that my presence gives hope to suffering people who believe I will tell their story and raise resources in Australia to give them a chance of surviving. I know that success will be limited. At best I will get an inadequate response and a polite hearing, but most Australians, who have not looked into these people's pleading eyes as I have done, will turn away. I know that the bubble we all live in is one where our immediate financial and familial worries are our reality. But I experience a form of survival guilt and feel I have failed the poorest and desperate after raising their hopes.

Only my faith keeps me trying to be open to pain and to not judge those who have not seen what I have seen.

Viktor Frankl, survivor of Auschwitz and author of *Man's Search for Meaning*, asked the question, 'Survived for what?' It's a valid question even for well-off Australians. Australia is the third-richest nation on earth, but we have widespread depression, an ice epidemic and our Indigenous population is not benefiting from the gains in life and health expectancy the rest of the population is experiencing. Although as a society we are massively affluent our youth suicide rate is among the highest in the world. One woman dies from family violence every week, and one in three Aussie women have experienced domestic violence. This is a much greater threat than terrorism, but it receives far fewer resources and is not prioritised.

Have we lost the meaning of true purpose and freedom? We have wonderful declarations about equality in the Universal Declaration of Human Rights. But they are not concrete, and are so often abused. I think the challenge is deeper than just educating about rights; we must engage our spiritual imagination to see that each individual is a spiritual citizen whose dignity is tied to our spiritual citizenship.

All sorted now

I thought I had the world sorted by the time I was twenty-four. I was fit and playing good football. I was just married and felt confident that I was set up for life in that regard. My faith was strong, and my career as a lawyer had begun a few years earlier; my legal firm had just offered me a lucrative partnership, and I knew I would be financially secure, if not wealthy. I was even sought out by my contemporaries for advice on living and seen as a sort of role model. I remember pontificating on how my faith could answer all doubts and meet all of life's exigencies. I even had the cheek to offer advice on parenting, despite not having kids yet. Believing that the few parenting books I had read made me an authority, I was critical of those in my circles who seemed to be daunted by their kids. (I remained confident of this expertise until I actually had children.)

In my spare time my wife, Merridie, and I led a young adults group that would see fifty people our age gathering for weekly meetings in our first matrimonial home, rented for that purpose because it had a huge lounge area. My self-esteem was bolstered by my relationship with one guy in our group, Andrew, who had come to the Christian faith through my influence. He had been doing some serious drugs, self-medicating his depression and living chaotically, but his conversion turned his life around. He was now clean, stable after stints in hospital for depression, and had a terrific gift as an encourager of others. He was also an amazing guitarist with a beautiful singing voice, and started writing haunting Dylan-esque songs about his new hope and faith.

After a year of Andrew's questions about God and the Bible — all answered with my usual self-assurance — I noticed he seemed a little less satisfied with our sessions and had withdrawn, so I made a time to catch up. But before that date he took a gun out to his garage and shot himself. I was utterly shattered. My faith had failed him. I obsessively retraced the answers I had given to his questions. They now seemed formulaic and hollow. I felt that I had failed him in my smugness and complacency.

I now know a lot more about mental illness, but at the time I framed it as a defect in my theology and faith. Andrew's suicide changed me. After a period of unsettledness I turned down the partnership in the legal firm I worked at, packed my bags and together my wife and I headed off to Switzerland to study theology in an international student community with African, Asian, American and European students. I desperately needed deeper answers.

One of the most influential subjects I did in my theology degree was on death and dying. Our lecturer asked us all to draw our personal time lines, citing our birthdates and proceeding with our educational, social and personal milestones. Then he asked us to write in the day and year we thought we would die. I was twenty-seven at the time so I wrote down 28 October 2025, when I would be seventy. It seemed old to me then. (Now as I recall my youthful rashness it gives me pause for thought. I did not think old people had much to offer but were an expensive health burden in their decline. Now nearing that stage, I fear the judgement of being economically useless.) That class exercise remains one of the most life-shaping exercises I have ever had. Instead of feeling indestructible, I realised that life is limited, a remarkable gift, and I wanted to live every day purposefully. And certainly now I want to outlive my early prediction!

I needed a spirituality that faced up to the problem of death, so that its heavy hand would not cripple or mock the meaning and purpose of my allotted number of days. By the end of my theological years in Switzerland I believed even more strongly in the resurrection. Jesus acted out the rule of God in his life and teaching and actions, welcoming all, even those who were seen as inferior, and he was resurrected. This is God's answer to exclusion and to malevolence.

The practical meaning of that belief is that it helps me to serve the people society might call losers, to be generous, to forgive others and to take risks. It frees me from the compulsion to live greedily — as if I must squeeze every experience, advancement and pleasure into this one life.

I discovered that many of my fellow believers would pick and choose when to take Jesus literally — usually preferring the culturally easy things but ignoring his explicit preaching of nonviolence and turning the other cheek.

William Wilberforce chose to focus on a culturally inconvenient teaching. He was attacked by Bible-believing Christians at the time for making the abolition of slavery central to his preaching of the Christian Gospel. His detractors pointed out that Jesus had said nothing explicitly about slavery and the Apostle Paul had sent back a runaway slave, Onesimus, to his master. The Gospel was a spiritual message and Wilberforce had complicated it with politics. Wilberforce had to go beneath the literal text of Scripture to the spirituality. There he understood that slaves were children of God just as much as he believed he himself was. They were his brothers and sisters and out of this evangelical spirituality the abolition bill was presented by him to Westminster in 1789.

As soon as I understood that every translation of the Bible is by definition an interpretation I understood that it was not literally dictated. Jesus spoke Aramaic and his teachings and story were first written down in Greek. When Erasmus put together the Greek manuscripts that form the Gospels and the New Testament in 1516 Christians were shocked to discover that it was not in the classical high Greek befitting a divinity, but in the rough common worker's Greek. That there were four Gospels meant that each writer had a diversity of central things they wanted to emphasise about the Jesus event. So did the other letters in the New Testament. This explained such a diversity of teachings and how different denominations elevated one teaching around which to form a church.

You may have concluded that my take on spirituality is all centred on the Bible. It is, but my interpretive key against difficult texts, such as those that seem to subjugate women (e.g. 'Let them not speak or teach a man'), is Jesus. I know it is circular logic, but the Gospels clearly show that he treated women as equals. They were the first witnesses to his resurrection in a culture where women could not give evidence in court. Likewise, the Apostle Paul even named one woman, Junia, as an apostle. And most of the earliest churches were all led by women. Whatever the difficult text, my interpretive key is how Jesus lived and the boundaries he smashed. He never quoted any of the nineteen 'Thou shalt nots' found in Leviticus, his Scriptures. He only quoted the one: 'Thou Shalt love your neighbour as yourself.' While understanding the Bible's message has been a large part of my working life and does preoccupy my thoughts much of the time, I know it is not the whole story.

I take inspiration

When it comes to my faith I think there have been outstanding examples and mentors who have helped shaped me and exemplified values I have wanted to embed in my own life. For the purposes of this book a few stories of people have come to mind — they are ordinary people whose lives have enriched mine; people who have made me reflect on the value of faith in facing the vicissitudes of life.

Living with purpose: Jani

Jani Von Wielligh was just twenty when she died in a car accident while on holiday in New Zealand in January 2015. She was a law student at Flinders University South Australia, and fluent in five languages. Apart from being brilliant she was passionate about justice for poor women. She volunteered tirelessly for World Vision at our stalls in shopping centres, promoting child sponsorship to help a poor community. Thanks to the negativity of our nation's political leaders, telling us we are all poor and victims, some people walk past the World Vision stalls, often shouting at volunteers that the money does not get to those in need and we should only look after ourselves. Where do those attitudes come from when we are living in the third-richest nation on earth and living in the greatest period of wealth ever in history?

Jani had an answer for those who bothered to listen, and often jolted them out of their prejudices. She would describe what she had seen and how she had personally visited the projects, and how she knew that the money gets there. She would describe the difference this had made in the lives of girls who have no chance just because they were born in the wrong place.

Jani would tell her mum at the end of each day how hard World Vision volunteering was, and how slim the generosity and optimism seemed to be, but then she'd recharge and go out the next day determined to make a difference.

Jani intended to be World Vision's CEO in the future. How do I know? Because she told me when I met her at an event in Adelaide that one day she wanted my job. I was thrilled, knowing the passion and brilliance she would bring. It was an honour to inspire someone like Jani with a dream for her future.

As I sat waiting for her funeral service in the Edge Church in Adelaide, I wept silently. Then I saw her parents, whom I had never met, standing in the front row. I expected them to be crumpled with grief, but they stood tall. As the communal singing that began the service started, I saw Jani's mother raise her hands to God in thankfulness for her daughter's life.

As I hugged Jani's parents after the funeral, they told me that they would try to deal with their grief by continuing Jani's passion for the poor through World Vision. As I write they have just raised $6000 as part of a Ride for Hope run by Edge Church. Even in the midst of their darkest moments they are caught up by Jani's passion. Though dead, she still lives.

Living with courage: Ross

My best mate is a tradesman named Ross. His trade is in fixing damaged baths and spas. We met in our early twenties when we were both involved in a local church and worked together leading the large group of young people that attended. Over the years we have played competition football and basketball together. We love our tennis, and as a doubles partner he makes me a winner. (He is a superb player.) We shared dreams in our twenties of living in community and so we all travelled to Europe: my wife and I studied theology in Switzerland, while Ross and his wife did a course at a community training centre in Holland. After that on their way home they spent a few years working on the hippie trail in Goa, India, rehabilitating druggies by providing a home and repatriating those in trouble.

We lived for many years in the St Kilda area, where we were all part of a church community. In the late 90s I was with Ross through the pain of his marriage breakdown, and some years later as a reverend I presided at his second wedding, even though there was one minor slip. Yes, I managed to call his new wife by the wrong name in the vows. Worse: I called her by the name of his first wife. Well, give me a break! That name had permanently fused in my mind as I had known them so well as a couple for twenty years. The congregation erupted in stifled sniggers while I tried to recover my footing, but this was just something from which there was no way back. God may forgive me but his lovely second wife, Sally, may find it harder. Ross just laughed, as if he was expecting me to stuff up something. But I have atoned since by doing the weddings of three of their shared daughters and getting all the names right!

Friendship is one of life's richest gifts. It needs few words and a glance conveys a world of meaning. I can live in my head and be too admiring of my own sophistication and eloquence. Ross is not like me in that regard, but a raised eyebrow or shake of the head is enough to bring me back to reality. Often crashing back. But trust developed over a long friendship means that even when it is critical it is never out of line. Like flint striking rock, so is friendship sharpening and disciplining.

We were photographed and interviewed for a magazine column a few years ago. Now, as a tradesman, Ross's gift lies in areas other than words. But he talked eloquently about being there for my wife and kids since I am away from home so much. I noticed a term he used, but I did not correct it at the time because I assumed the journalist knew what Ross meant. Well, this journo was of the literal transcribing school, and when the article came out I heard Merridie scream from the kitchen table. I came downstairs quickly, to find her looking mortified. She pointed out that Ross had described his role in our family as the 'de facto husband'. I knew he meant to say de facto father to my kids, particularly my sporty sons, but there it stood in unambiguous print for all to see. So I guess the scales are nicely balanced, with both our wives bearing ill will towards us for word slips.

Friendship is for better or worse; that is what makes it friendship. It is not a score card of reciprocal favours and debts. It is unconditional or it is not true friendship. Sporty, fun-loving Ross coughed and sneezed violently two years ago for a few weeks in winter. He had a bit of pneumonia, but so close are the margins in his business that he kept working. When Ross repetitively coughed he dislodged a disc in his neck, and by the time he got to a specialist he was very close to being a quadriplegic. He had lost the ability to walk stably, and the nerves in his fingers were so shot he could barely write or hold a pen. Now, a year and more later, after two major operations and intensive therapy, he is walking but may never play tennis again. Even holding a racquet is hard. And all this for a man with a collection of over a hundred new and antique racquets.

Even more confronting was the economic setback, as he could not pursue his trade and, as a sole operator, he had to sell his business at a fire sale price. Despite all these devastating knocks for such an active, generous-hearted guy, he remains positive. He has to undertake extended physio but is now also using his time to mentor others with disabilities, and working to build community for people with mental illnesses.

Our friendship (without tennis) remains just as strong, and will continue to do so — that is, as long as he remembers which de facto role he is playing!

Living with loss: Lillian

Another friend, Lillian, struggled for years with her drug-addicted son David. He was a talented musician but could not shake the heroin. His manipulation of Lillian when he needed to score was so demoralising that for eight months she had to cut all contact with him to protect herself. But she would occasionally ring me and ask that I take some food to him, as she worried that he might not be eating. She has two other wonderful children but, as any parent who has been here knows, the one in trouble sucks all the oxygen out of life and prevents you from really enjoying the others.

One night David and his girlfriend were crossing a road when a car came out of nowhere. David selflessly pushed his girlfriend out of the way, saving her life, and his body took the full impact. He was rendered a quadriplegic and was unconscious on life support. Lilly was at his bedside every day for months. Despite his survival being touch and go for a while, he lived. With the payout from the accident, after spending a year in hospital, he bought a house equipped for a quadriplegic.

Lilly moved in and for the next three and half years nursed David day and night. She had her son back.

This was a time for David's brokenness to find some wholeness. With a pen in his mouth he wrote some of his best poems and songs. The family relationships were slowly restored and he brought healing to many around him. He took responsibility for how he had been living. After having been estranged from his siblings for years when he was doing drugs, now that he was finally clean he attended both his siblings' weddings. I officiated at both. But the congestion in his lungs was always terrible and slowly his condition deteriorated to the point where he lost his battle. He died at peace and well loved.

Funerals are always hard for me, and to lead this one, having been so personally involved, was no exception. But there were also many things to be thankful about. Lilly seemed to be coping, but it is always the months after that are the hardest. Lilly was living alone in the house where keeping David alive had been her occupation, day and night. She felt totally empty and had no meaning now that she was not nursing him, and could find no reason to live herself. She later told me that she had been watching the video of David's funeral every night for months. One night it was all too much: she overdosed on sleeping tablets. At 5 am, feeling she was losing consciousness, she rang me to thank me for all I had done, to say goodbye and to ask me to pray for her soul, as she would be at peace soon. It was meant to be a goodbye message for my voicemail, not a cry for help. She was resolved to go and be with David.

It was lucky not only that my phone was on, but also that I was awake. I was actually up at the time as I had been vomiting because of a bug I had picked up in Myanmar while responding to a cyclone a few weeks before. I jumped in the car and sped to her house some forty-five minutes away. Before I left I rang another friend, as in my illness I just could not remember Lilly's street address for the ambulance, though I knew how to drive there. En route I had to stop on a major bridge and get out as another vomiting attack assailed me. I was incredibly relieved to see the ambulance in the driveway as I pulled up. They had broken in and were soon carrying her out, unconscious, on a stretcher. I remember feeling relieved when I saw that her face was not covered.

Since that desperate day Lilly has rebuilt her meaning through her Slavic Orthodox faith, friends and family. She has taken great joy in her first grandchild and has taken in boarders who have become best friends. She throws the most sumptuous dinner parties followed by dancing at home. She is very much alive and engaged with others.

Part of the healing work she had to undertake was recognising that David would not have wanted her to die, and so the choice she had taken was neither honouring his wishes nor those of her other kids, let alone caring for herself. She has learned to trust life and God again despite her scars.

Blessing others: Basil

One of the finest singing voices I have heard belonged to a man called Basil Swanton. He had a divine baritone. I remember an American opera singer attending a service at the city church where I was a minister. The singer was in between his shows and heard Basil singing behind him in the congregation. He told me that Basil's voice could make its owner millions, so rare and sublime was it.

Basil died early last year at the age of ninety-eight. I was overseas, but my wife went to the funeral. Basil was such a humble, godly man that, although I had been his minister, I knew little about him. A more complete picture of him came out at the funeral. I knew an unmarried man, tall, who stood with a ramrod-straight back. A man who was a manager and financial planner for a wealthy philanthropist. I knew a man who was personally generous to the street mission of homeless people and drug addicts called Urban Seed that began during my tenure as minister at the church.

I did not know that he rose at 5 am each day to pray. I did not know that all his life he refused to own a telephone, car or television, living as simply as he could so as to give as much as possible away. His one luxury was a small transistor radio so he could listen to the news and current affairs, which would inform his prayers. He was very well informed.

Basil was a survivor. He had followed his older brother in enlisting in the army in World War II, but his mother forced him to withdraw. Terrified of losing two sons, she begged him to do something safer. So he immediately signed up for the air force. Tragically, his brother, Stuart, died a few short years later after being a prisoner of war to the Japanese on Ambon Island.

I never got to ask Basil how much his countercultural simplicity and generosity was a response to his surviving and his brother dying. But to learn more after his death I felt humbled.

I do pray but as an activist and an extrovert it is the hardest work I do. Silence is not natural for me, but I still try. When people ask me what I pray about, I think of the story of the Jewish man at the Wailing Wall in Jerusalem. He was known for his piety because he was there every day for hours, his body rocking in prayer. When they asked him what he was praying about he said, 'Peace between Jews and Palestinians, reduction and abolition of nuclear weapons, the end of racist attacks and prosperity for the poor.'

'Wow,' they said, 'and are your prayers working?'

'Well, no,' he said, 'I sometimes feel like I'm talking to a brick wall!'

Yeah, I've been there too. But when I think of the calm, the generosity, integrity and simplicity of the life of Basil in this frenetic society, I sense his prayers made a difference.

PART VI

Bringing the outsiders in

Change of heart

Pastor Christy Buckingham and her husband, Rob, are ministers who live their faith. Australia was riveted by their years-long journey with two convicted drug traffickers, Andrew Chan and Myuran Sukumaran. Sadly, these young Australian men were executed by the Indonesians in 2015 after ten years in a Bali prison.

Who would spend time with criminal thugs like them? Christy and Rob (among others) did. The resulting journey to faith transformed not just the boys themselves, but also a number of their fellow inmates. Andrew Chan completed a full theological degree online, under Christy and Rob's supervision, to become a better pastor to the inmates that he supported — foreign and Indonesian. He gave hope to so many that some prisoners offered to die in his place so that he would be able to keep up his good work. He got accredited as a minister, regularly led services in prison, and got married just before being executed. Myuran Sukumaran, a painter, inspired and mentored other prisoners. The lives of a good number of inmates of Kerobokan Prison, a hotbed of drugs and violence, were transformed by these guys.

It was a story of redemption that touched the nation. We did not want them to die. Their journey spoke to the brokenness in all of our lives and the possibility of wholeness and a second chance. We grieved as a nation when they sang 'Amazing Grace' on the way to the execution site, refused the blindfold to show solidarity, and were executed.

Andrew Chan used the last forty-eight hours of his life to counsel and pray with the others on Death Island who were to be executed with him and Myuran. Myuran had developed in Kerobokan Prison a phenomenal artistic skill — his friend and mentor Ben Quilty said of him, 'In my life I've only ever seen one other artist make this seismic progress of such a dizzying pace'— and in the last forty-eight hours, which one might think would be paralysing, he kept up this pace and finessed his work with four last paintings. His lawyer, Julian McMahon, carried them out after the execution. One was a picture of Myuran's own heart: a symbol of hope, but also a terrible reminder of the executioner's task.

But the hearts of Australian politicians and public have been profoundly changed by this story of redemption and rehabilitation. This is the same group of people who had no 'in principle' problem with the death penalty only a few years before. Our politicians, in a remarkable display of bipartisanship, realised that you cannot be selective when it comes to the death penalty. We saw that state-sanctioned murder is devastating to our humanity, for while there is still life there is the hope of redemption — even in prison.

Although there is a new commitment to this principle, it will of course be tested by the next obscene crime and the demands for retribution it will bring. It will be tested by our economic interests, when our biggest trading partners — the US, Japan and China — still practise the death penalty.

But for now we have reacquainted ourselves with the injustices of capital punishment. That DNA evidence has liberated so many wrongly convicted people from death row, and that executed prisoners are disproportionately black, exposes the racism and injustice of the death penalty. The ineffectiveness of the death penalty as a deterrent has been widely proven, with US states that carry the death penalty suffering from *higher* murder rates than those that don't. But more tellingly, it reminds us that, when it comes to retribution, only God should have the power of life and death. We can and must punish offenders, but no state or human authority can carry the ultimate sanction.

For all this, I am thankful for the lives of Andrew Chan and Myuran Sukumaran; their deaths touched the heart of a nation.

What makes a man

I was in the Solomon Islands a few years ago to observe our three-day workshop called Channels of Hope. It addresses domestic violence. The Solomons has the highest rate of reported domestic violence in the world. Because it is a Christian nation and churches are the trusted institution, this workshop was conducted for all the Anglican bishops, including the archbishop. The World Vision leaders were a Zambian woman and a male staffer from Zimbabwe. They began by asking the bishops to draw a picture of what makes a man a man and a woman a woman in their culture. The archbishop held his picture up first. The man had a spear in his hand: he was a warrior, and he was kicking obstacles out of his way with his leg. A man, he explained, is brave, he leads and he overcomes obstacles. Then he held up his picture of a woman. She had a massive tongue curled around many times as it came out of her mouth. A woman in this culture gossips, interferes and creates problems, he explained. Men have to fix this. He added, 'This is why women need to be disciplined.' As others spoke, I heard that discipline includes a cuff over the head if dinner is late, if she's been gossiping or has not been working long enough in the garden.

The next question was: So what is the place of a woman in God's creation as compared to Adam? As serious students of the Bible, all hands went up. The men confidently knew the biblical answer. They jumped straight to Genesis 2:21: the creation of woman from Adam's rib while he slept. Throughout history, the implications of this interpretation have been devastating, as it portrays women as only derived from man, and merely from his rib at that. So obviously she is inferior and derivative; he's the important one, and submission and service of him is her lot. But well before this text, in Genesis 1:27, it reads:

so God created mankind in his own image, in the image of God he created them; male and female he created them and God blessed them and invited both fill the earth and subdue and sustain it.

There are women in the original creation, equal with men, equally given authority to rule and also sharing the image of God. As the leaders explained this, I watched the bishops' eyes open wider as the implications of their oversight sank in. As the day unfolded, more problematic texts that seemed to relegate women were discussed and the men responded with shock that they had never seen that women were indubitably equal in identity and status.

Towards the end of the first day, after discussing whether women needed to be disciplined and treated the way they were in a culture that considered itself simultaneously warrior and Christian, one bishop started silently weeping, his shoulders shuddering and chest heaving. Our facilitators stopped and asked him to express his feelings. He sobbed through his tears that he had just realised that he was an abuser. Silence filled the room and then hearts were unlocked as others agreed he was not alone.

After three days of Bible study modelled by a black man and a black woman sharing the leadership and teaching, and after much discussion about differences in gender roles and male authority, each man was asked to draw a picture of what makes a man and a woman in God's eyes. Dramatically different pictures were sketched — pictures of equality and respect. Difficult patriarchal passages of scripture were relativised by the transcendent truth that God is male *and* female, and to believe we are made in his image is to understand that dignity. There is no warrant for male superiority.

Of course, my nation has had a wakeup call with the discovery that one woman dies every week at the hands of her male partner. Domestic violence is a much greater risk than terrorism, yet terrorism attracts a lot more funding. Rosie Batty, whose former partner killed their thirteen-year-old son, has undertaken a remarkable journey of forgiveness and advocacy for the silent victims, culminating in her being made the Australian of the Year for 2015. Her advocacy has paid off, with government funding to tackle the scourge and take a national program seriously.

We have a huge way to travel to change mindsets about women. So many females were aborted under the one-child policy in China that there is now a deficit of 200 million girls. With no brides for Chinese men, there has been greater female trafficking from neighbouring Nepal and Myanmar. In other parts of the world girls are still pulled out of school by fathers to do the labour of collecting wood and water, which is not expected of boys, and in India we know that a woman gets raped every minute, with perpetrators rarely getting punished because girls have so little status or power. Of course, in the developed world we still struggle to pay women equally.

And with more women in the workforce, men have not picked up their game to fill the gap in domestic care. Someone still has to cook and clean, care for children and supervise their homework, turn nurse when family members are sick or attend to elderly parents. Yes, the wealthy can subcontract much of this care out, but most of us with both parents in the workforce juggle a massive care deficit. The gender power struggle to share family duties is real, as society programs men to protect and provide, so they struggle to find meaning in domesticity. But we need to step up.

Women and purity

When women are protected by their families, it is often for the wrong reasons. In so much of the world today, part of male protection is to ensure the purity of a daughter so she doesn't become 'soiled goods'. Any questions about a daughter's purity can become a family shame and an economic disaster when negotiating a bride price. Early marriage and female genital mutilation (FGM) are reminders to girls that their sexuality is to be controlled. There are various grades of FGM, but in places such as Somalia a brutal and extreme form is practised by sewing up girls' vaginas to ensure at marriage there is proof of virginity. We in World Vision respect culture, but challenge anything that treats women as inferior. We reject the relativism that considers culture untouchable when that culture doesn't honour women's rights. We do it sensitively, but we always try to change the software in men's brains that treats women as impure and inferior. We do Channels of Hope in West Africa with imams using the Qur'an to counteract domestic violence and patriarchy. Again it is using their texts and sensitively noting differences in belief.

Interestingly, World Vision, as a Christian organisation, is often more easily accepted in other cultures than secular development organisations. Many people in the developing world associate religion with having a culture, and think that secular society means you have no culture. I've had people ask me how secular people name a child or have a wedding if they have no religion.

We only hear terrible news from Afghanistan, and how the Taliban are back. But there is much good news where World Vision are working in Western Afghanistan. The mullahs are the gatekeepers for ideas and culture. We have trained over 380 mullahs and 1800 community leaders through Channels of Hope in Gender and Islam. These programs cover child protection, mother and child health and celebrating families, emphasising how families cannot function without equality for girls and dignity for women. When we asked the religious head of the mullahs how he felt about working with a Christian organisation he responded, 'We prayed that someone would come and help with our families and Allah sent you. You are the answer to our prayer.'

Both cultural and religious notions of holiness and purity sit behind the subjugation of women. In 1084, Pope Gregory VII ruled that Catholic priests would have to be celibate. Before then, they could marry — so what caused the change? In part it was losing Church properties left to the children of priests. But it was also the belief that women were unclean, so the same hands that touched a woman could not hold the holy wine and bread in the Eucharist. This taboo seems to persist to this day, as Republican presidential candidate Donald Trump seemed to still have trouble with bleeding women in 2015.

Jesus scandalised the religious leaders of his day by including women in his circle, breaking bread with 'loose' women and being touched by bleeding women. His behaviour offended their understanding of a holy God.

Saul the Pharisee (who became the Apostle Paul) was first a persecutor of Christians, because a crucified Messiah was an insult to his God of life who would have no contact with death. Imagine the shock of his religious conversion where on the Damascus road he had a vision of Jesus raised to the Messiah's place at the right hand of God. His version of a Holy God was overturned. The rules had changed and purity as a category was abolished. Only after this conversion could Paul write the revolutionary words, 'in Christ neither male nor female, neither Jew nor Gentile, slave or free'. He could easily have added 'clean or unclean'.

Tragically, the notion of female uncleanness has stayed strong. In the developing world a major block to girls' education is sanitation issues and the cost of a school providing the privacy and protection required for their needs.

In many Arab and developing nations female purity is so fetishised, and the lack of it so terribly punished, that unmarried women are regularly murdered or disfigured by acid attacks so their physical disfigurement advertises their uncleanness.

One Indian survivor, named Laxmi, was scarred at sixteen by an acid attack. From day one after the attack, Laxmi refused to hide her face. She was the first survivor to do so. Her campaign to stop acid being sold over any grocery store counter was backed by the Indian Supreme Court. She has given courage to many other survivors.

The biggest problem facing Africa?

My friends Ridley and Mieke Bell from Lismore in northern New South Wales have become generous supporters of World Vision. They have invested in northern Uganda, up towards the South Sudan border, some five hours' drive from the capital, Kampala. It is in an area where World Vision works and where the Bells met a brave nurse called Conny. She was delivering babies with a torch in her mouth because there was no electricity, and the pregnant mothers had to sleep on the dirt floor because the little health outstation had no bed or even mattresses. Conny, who is married to a local farmer, was overwhelmed with the need. Over sixteen women die in childbirth every day in Uganda, and the majority of these deaths take place in the north, which is the region ravaged by Joseph Kony's Lord's Resistance Army. It is the poorest area of a poor nation. Mieke is also a nurse, and she was so moved by Conny's courage and commitment that she and Ridley asked what the area needed.

Twelve months later we were back and World Vision Uganda, through the Bells' generosity, had built and opened a twenty-five bed hospital. Now fifty babies a month are being delivered there, and they and their mothers are surviving. When we met Conny she was at work looking spotless in her white nurse's uniform and bonnet. She was nursing a baby boy, her own baby, born in the intervening twelve months. She had proudly named him Ridley. Over a thousand people, all poor farmers, had walked many kilometres in the heat of the day to be at the hospital for the opening. The dancing, speeches and feasting at the opening were so life-giving. World Vision had also put in a playground, and hearing the laughter of the kids who had never seen, let alone been on, a swing, slide or seesaw was a delight. They were having a ball.

Back in Kampala on the following Sunday we went to St David's Cathedral for a Sunday service. The cathedral hosted five services a day, and there were queues to get in, so we were excited to be in a vital, dynamic faith community. Watching a robed Anglican clergywoman lead the congregation in joyous singing and dancing was unforgettable.

But then the bishop leading the service asked that all the children under fourteen leave, as the sermon was not suitable for young people. Intriguing. A medical doctor from Addis Ababa was the guest preacher. He began well. 'I want to talk about the two greatest threats facing Africa.'

I whispered to Ridley, 'Probably corruption and maybe war or terrorism.' We had had to pass through airport-type security grids to just get into the church service, so real is the threat of terrorism. But I was wrong.

The two greatest threats, according to this man, were abortion and homosexuality. He proceeded to explain why, with graphic depictions of anal sex thrown up on the white cathedral walls as evidence. He preached with full force against these 'unnatural acts'. People were gasping with shock. I was shifting in my seat and looking for an escape, but the church was packed to the rafters. I remember Ridley looking pale and turning to me, whispering, 'Tim, am I really in church looking at this?' This was not our idea of uplifting worship! I looked around and wondered how many gay people might be sitting silently in the service and feeling threatened. What would Jesus, who broke down purity boundaries, think? How could gay people survive, let alone reconcile their sexuality, with such condemnation? Thankfully the sermon finished and the final hymn was announced. Ironically, it was the rocking, upbeat 'Oh Happy Day'. In surreal rhythmic time we rocked out.

Throughout Africa and the developing world I think homophobia is the result of a purity taboo that homosexual acts are 'unnatural', entrenched in social disgust and legislation. In many nations like Uganda, it is not just homosexual acts but also orientation that is criminalised. President Obama cut Uganda's aid for not repealing these laws. To accept that gay people are not just evil hedonists or worse, child abusers, but can express real love and monogamous commitment (and of course promiscuity, just like heterosexuals) is difficult for some traditional cultures. African leaders like Archbishop Desmond Tutu has described homophobia as a 'crime against humanity' and 'every bit as unjust as apartheid'. Accommodating pluralism and modernity is a challenge for both African indigenous culture and the wider church that wishes to be faithful to its traditions: Muslim, Christian or Australian Indigenous.

There is no escaping the difficult conclusion that the ancient world and the worldview of the Bible thought homosexuality unnatural. The Bible knows nothing of love or marriage between the same sex. When the Apostle Paul says in Romans that 'men have abandoned the natural relations with women and were inflamed with lust for one another and committed shameful acts with other men', it is true that he may have been targeting not homosexuality but pederasty, which was widespread in the Greco-Roman world. Even so, at no point does Scripture make the case for same sex relationships as a norm. Mind you, neither does the Bible esteem romantic love and a lot of the notions we assume as the basis of marriage today; it was more concerned with covenantal faithfulness in marriage and its relationship to God.

Today most young people in the West (including in churches) accept that sexuality is on a spectrum between total heterosexuality at one end and total homosexuality at the other, with a whole range in between. So they see it as natural to accept a range of sexual orientations and not label one as aberrant or unnatural. Many also believe this is an issue of gospel values: of bringing the outsider in. But for others in the developing world and among many older people in the West, the boundaries between natural and unnatural (and therefore wrong) are very fixed. They see this as an issue of truth. It is not obvious how we reconcile these views, and I have seen within the global World Vision community the anguish that this debate can create.

I think this will be a major generational challenge in the developing world. There are ways to move the debate forward: for example, thinking through how the Bible elevates fidelity; encouraging faithfulness and commitment in relationships, whether heterosexual or between gay LGBT couples (who are going to pair off, whatever the law's or society's preferences), and reflecting on how we should resist the notion sexuality is what defines us. Sexuality is just one strand in a personality: why should it become a person's defining feature? But watching the reaction in that church that morning, I knew there was a long way to travel.

Homosexuality remains a difficult issue for the Church to navigate, even in the developed world. But this is not the first time the Church has confronted complicated and deeply contested debates! A starting point is that people hear each other respectfully, and understand that others have deep convictions. Second, there should be no scope for homophobia or prejudice against minorities (the outsiders). But we should remember that homosexual practice is firmly regarded as unnatural by many diverse traditions. This needs to be respected whether it is based on cultural beliefs or religious conviction. People of faith will not surrender what they believe is a matter of fidelity to Scripture.

This is why I suspect it will take generational change until a consensus emerges, backed by anthropological evidence, about faithfulness and the diverse human spectrum of sexuality and so what is considered natural or unnatural.

When speaking in early 2015 at a pastors' conference in Australia on leadership, I said, 'I'm not here to talk today about the issue of gay marriage. But I want to say that surely, as Christians, we celebrate that gays have been able to come out of the shadows of shame, stigma and criminalisation to enjoy acceptance.' I added that less stigma means fewer young gays being bullied or committing suicide, which is surely a cause to celebrate. Spontaneous applause followed from the younger pastors. But after I had finished some of the older pastors took me aside and chastised me. They disagreed with my sentiments, and one even said that my comments were dangerously interfering with God's judgement on immoral, unnatural behaviour. It reminded me of the attitudes of some churches to HIV/AIDS in the 1980s, that the virus was evidence of God's judgement on that behaviour. I do not remember anyone using that logic by saying that lung cancer is God's judgement on smokers! Sadly, that thinking still pops up. (One Pentecostal pastor had said in 2009 that the terrible Black Saturday Victorian bushfires, which claimed 180 lives, were due to that state government's abortion laws.)

From what I have seen in many different cultures, we are likely to live with this debate for a long time to come. But that does not mean that the debate cannot change, as it did with HIV/AIDS in the early 2000s. Not long after I had joined World Vision, I remember seeing our US team conduct a fifty-state tour of churches to challenge wrong-headed attitudes towards HIV and God's judgement. This battling of repressive purity laws with grace and compassion was worthy of the teachings of Jesus, and helped make possible the US government's support for retrovirals that saved the lives of more than a million people.

Dopes

I am a lifelong supporter of the Essendon Australian Rules football club. As a child I loved the exhilaration of playing in my red striped Essendon jumper, sporting on my back the number of my favourite star player. As an adult I go as a spectator in my red-and-black colours, sing the song, hate the opposition and their supporters and express all the rituals of tribal worship. And I love talking with Essendon fans about our performance, chances at the premiership and the details of the latest hamstring injury that threatens our world.

It has been an excruciating time to be a supporter, as the club and my football heroes have been engulfed in a drugs storm since 2012. I have had second thoughts about supporting them this year. Essendon, a Melbourne suburban team, and its thirty-four players are the first team to have been found guilty by the World Anti-Doping Court. The players have been suspended for twelve months. This has stretched my emotions and caused untold stress and pain in the lives of Essendon supporters. Yes, I admit to coming back from a humanitarian disaster and poring over the newspapers I missed for every football detail and development in this court saga. It's that important to me!

But, though passionate that the players should have been cleared of these charges, I am troubled. I know that if I, as CEO of World Vision, told my staff I needed better performance from them and decreed they were to go offsite and get injections away from the club doctor, signing a release form claiming that it was their decision and not mine, and if I added that, by the way, I cannot tell you exactly what is being injected into your body, then I do not think I would still be in my CEO job. Neither would it say much about the calibre of my staff if they obeyed!

Yet all of this happened at Essendon in that year. In my head I know this to be totally unethical. Its motto was 'whatever it takes', and it did just that to get an advantage. A sporting institution embarked on an experimental pharmacology program and kept it secret. How can I support them when the best defence Essendon had was 'we're sure they weren't injected with performance-enhancing drugs, but since we lost or destroyed the medical records we can't tell you what drugs they took'? Yes, that was actually Essendon's best defence! But tribe is so strong that even though my head says I should walk away and find another team to support, I just can't do it. I continue to go in my red-and-black and cheer at games and get swept up in all the emotions each week.

The strange clash in my emotions was heightened by a resentment that the World Anti-Doping Agency (WADA) were now going to try my football heroes. How ridiculous! Sure, Russians and the Chinese have been drug cheats and should be pursued by an unbiased international body, but not Aussie footballers. We're honest! Keep WADA for nations who are likely to cheat, not us Australians.

The global village first described by Marshall McLuhan in the 1960s did not bring global harmony. McLuhan later described it more as a global theatre than a village. In a global world we all watch the same play performed on the stage but, because we sit in the dark, we do not notice that we are having totally different reactions. Some love it, others are offended and, because we never talk and only leave with the friends we came in with, we leave assuming everyone had our reaction. We fail to understand the culture and bias we brought to the play that might explain different reactions. We are intolerant when others do not see it our way when they saw the same thing. This in-group bias is true of all groups and it's what makes international rules so necessary as a forum where we sort out the bias.

Now that I have got that anger out, do I have any solutions? Well, the best way to face our in-group bias is to trust the diversity of international bodies and rules.

Addiction

I have spent a lot of my working life with addicts. One of the things I worked out pretty soon was, after rehabilitation, there were only two things I needed to ask in order to predict whether they would stay clean or be back. The first was 'Do you have a job?' and the second was 'Do you have friends who are not using drugs?' If either was lacking it was a good chance they would be back. If both were missing I knew that they would soon be using again. I was rarely wrong. It's the same for prisoners leaving prison. The same two questions are almost all you need to ask to predict recidivism. I would add that a faith commitment can also be an extra protection.

Many who work in the field have puzzled over the fact that some users of hard drugs (only about 15 per cent) are hopeless addicts and yet others can use and control the substance (or the slot machines or the alcohol). Why? Professor Bruce Alexander explored addiction by experimenting on rats. The rats would have two sources of water: one plain, the other laced with an opiate. The rats always preferred the drugged water and would eventually kill themselves.

Alexander then refined the rats' habitats, placing

the rats in cages with the two types of water, but also with other rats and cheese and toys. He discovered that the rats under these conditions hardly ever chose to drink the drugged water or overdosed. Given play and company they were not interested in dulling the pain. Based on similar theories, Portugal, which had a huge drug problem, diverted spending on punishment for drug offenders to social rehabilitation in the community and job sponsorship. With community and jobs and social connections, drug offenders dramatically turned around their drug problems. People need a wider meaning in community to survive in a healthy state.

Again it is my faith that still gives me the best working hypothesis. It teaches me that we are created good, not evil or malevolent. But there was a fall from this state as we exercised our freedom negatively, and this 'fall' left a fundamental fracture in our character and behaviour. Sex is good and exhilarating, but this fundamental fracture means it can be enveloped by lust, pornography and betrayal. Work is good and grants purpose, but it can be the site of bullying, abuse and, at the extreme end, slavery. Families are the primary unit to teach, support and equip humans to live functional lives. But they can also be the site of incest, domestic violence and verbal and emotional abuse. Markets are usually much better than governments in maximising freedom of choice and ensuring the efficient allocation and distribution of resources, but when markets lack transparency and are captured by vested interests they lead to corruption and inequality.

I do not understand why some people, communities and nations remain trapped in brokenness. We all know that, whatever the wrong done to us, bitterness and a refusal to forgive cripples us as much as the wrongdoer who hurt us. I see inter-communal hatred and conflict where the participants have forgotten the original cause, yet generations later they are still hating and fighting. One of the founders of the IRA was a Protestant and is buried in a Protestant church in Dublin. He was seeking Irish political independence from the British. All too soon this nationalist political liberation agenda was turbo-charged as a sectarian Catholic–Protestant battle. They had forgotten that it had nothing to do with religion, and terrible hatred and religious violence, neighbour on neighbour, followed for generations. I see national stagnation where leaders can name causes like economic unfairness, injustice or blatant corruption but seem utterly unable to move forward and deal with these paralysing issues.

My faith gives me some clues but still I am not clear why some people are able to transcend terrible brokenness and become whole. Why some communities and nations deal with these obstacles better and even overcome them and move on to prosperity and stability and others do not. But I do know that faith helps. Nelson Mandela certainly drew on that spiritual resource. No one in the world believed that apartheid in South Africa could be dismantled without revolution, let alone that South Africa could manage to hold free elections without massive bloodshed and payback after the bitterness of apartheid. One man, Nelson Mandela, inspired in part by his Methodist faith, rose above hatred and left prison without a trace of bitterness or the need to seek revenge for his imprisonment of twenty-seven years. He led the nation through a relatively peaceful transition and formed a multi-racial rainbow democracy promising that whites would be welcome. In a powerful act of symbolism, he donned the Springbok jumper — a sporting symbol of white racism and sporting oppression — at the Rugby World Cup. And the white Springboks won the World Cup and the rainbow nation celebrated together.

PART VII

The place for faith

The one true thing

Over the years, I have been struck by how many times, when we get to the pointy end of a difficult decision, someone shouts out in frustration, 'Oh, for f#ck's sake!' Most people present do not bat an eyelid, as it is now so common a cry. Everyone knows it comes from exasperation and is simply a desperate attempt to cut through the tedious quibbling and resolve the argument. It's the ultimate plea for common sense.

Sometimes in these contexts someone might remember I am a reverend and quickly apologise for their language. After a moment of uneasy silence I usually say, 'Well, I have heard the word before.' The debate usually then moves on to some sort of a resolution.

In an oversexualised world perhaps I should not be surprised how this phrase has become de rigueur in all types of settings. Of course comedians and actors in films have long dropped the f-word and now television seems to have embraced it as a word acceptable in mainstream entertainment. My point is not about the change of manners itself, but the culture shift behind the change. Once upon a time our last appeal may have been 'Oh, for God's sake', an appeal to decency or truth.

We had commonly held values and they were connected to a faith system, whether it was personally believed or not. We argued our ideas with an appeal to our ultimate understanding of that commonly recognised faith: for God's sake.

Not now. The shift has been subtle, but in exasperation it is now to the most private and intimate act that we appeal. But what is the culture change in this?

To say 'For f#ck's sake' is to appeal to the fundamental biological act by which we all started life. In that act, our destiny is set. In our inherited genes lie our health and longevity; in some latitudes to be born a woman or into the lower castes means opportunities will be limited. In other cases an embryo may end up part of a royal family. All because of what can appear to be a random biological union.

This exposes a world view that the fact of our existence is the only true thing we know about ourselves; it's the one thing we can appeal to. If the world began spontaneously without purpose and may end spontaneously without warning, we must face that we are alone.

But few of us can or do live like this. Whatever the indisputable science of physics has laid down, we struggle to find in this approach a purpose and ethic or a way to live. If we are to find significance and meaning, we must go beyond science to faith and spirituality. We all trust something that we cannot prove. We all live by faith. By that I mean we cannot prove that the purpose or the ethics that undergird our lives are scientifically right and given, yet we all make a leap of faith or adopt some intuitive spirituality to live with some meaning that we have to trust and nurture.

I have visited Auschwitz and a few other concentration camps. At Auschwitz I thought about Viktor Frankl, the Austrian neurologist and psychiatrist and a contemporary of Sigmund Freud. Frankl survived Auschwitz, that place of horror, by realising that even in the midst of death and barbarity his guards could not rob him of a personal space to meditate on love and beauty. They could control his labour and movements — even his very life and death — but they could not control his mind. This was a tiny free space where he, not his SS guards, might exercise control. His best-selling book, *Man's Search for Meaning*, was written fourteen years after he miraculously survived.

Of course, in those years Frankl asked, 'Will I survive?' But after liberation and finding that so many of his family, friends and fellow Jews had been murdered he found his question became, 'So I survived, but survived for what?'

This was an even more difficult question. Perhaps only in extremis does the magnitude of that question resonate so profoundly. Those of us who have never faced great threats to our existence and live safe and pedestrian lives may never anguish over this. But the question remains: Living for what? What is our life's meaning in the midst of the challenges we face? There is no textbook answer. And ultimately there will be a faith dimension to however we answer that and however we choose to live.

As the poet Cyprian Norwid said,

To be what is called happy, one should have (1) something to live on, (2) something to live for, (3) something to die for. The lack of one of these results in drama. The lack of two results in tragedy.

I believe there is no easy escape from this universal human task. Those who try to escape invariably turn to alcohol, drugs or amnesia. Nor can it be contracted out to self-help gurus' easy answers if life is to be authentic and joyful. Many confuse the pursuit of 'something to live on' as an end in itself. But there is ample testimony that, once your physical needs are met, greater wealth does not lead to greater happiness.

Most meet the 'something to live for' requirement with family, community and even their nation. This is a good answer, but still not necessarily sufficient. Nationalism can lead to war and families and communities often fragment.

The most difficult question to answer is 'something to die for'. It is no accident that all our greatest heroes seemed to embrace this challenge — which is why they inspire us. It is why we teach their stories to our young. Go to Saint Paul's Cathedral and at the west entrance you will see the statues of Maximilian Kolbe, Martin Luther King and Dietrich Bonhoeffer, among others: twelve modern martyrs in total carved in stone.

Another way to frame this question is to ask, 'What do I worship?' It is the clue to sorting out what we are prepared to die for. Mary Gilmore was an Australian political utopian and a poet and activist. She went to Paraguay to join a socialist community and believed that the capitalist reduction of everything to money defeated the teachings of Jesus Christ. She came back and founded the Lyceum Club for women in Melbourne. In *The Rue Tree* she wrote,

> *The need of humanity is to lift its heart to something not wholly contained within itself … Man must worship something. Secular, religious, or the toss of the coin, he makes a choice.*

I believe with her that we all incurably need to worship. It is a statement of what ultimately matters — enough even to die for. People will worship sex, money, power or something else that ultimately matters. In a religious sense I see this worship in the millions of young people now flocking to Pentecostal churches in the developing world of Africa and Latin America and raising their voices courageously against dictators and corruption.

I understand the preparedness to die for family or nation but query whether we should worship them. Being and existence is sacred, but for me it needs to be deeper. I worship the God whose image is stamped in all of life's existence and all of humanity but particularly the poor (which is most of the world). My faith is not simply a recipe for me to flourish in this life. When I worship by saying 'your will be done on earth', I know its true meaning is that it may require a costly sacrifice — even the ultimate sacrifice. Faith is not just a formula for success and flourishing that can be abandoned if difficult! It is deeper than happiness and speaks to identity and conviction, whatever the cost.

This is expressed in my World Vision work when I go to war zones and disasters. World Vision is mainly seen by our donors as trying to answer the first question, by giving people something to live on; but our vision includes the other two questions. Our motto is 'For every child life in all its fullness. Our prayer for every heart — the will to make it so.' That is something to live for and to die for.

'What are humans that you are mindful of them?'

A hallmark of secularism is the belief that science has indeed answered these meaning questions with greater precision than religious fairy tales. Is science not a better explanation of why we are here than faith in God or a fuzzy intuitive spirituality?

Certainly many religious beliefs have had to retreat in the face of scientific discoveries. Most famously, Galileo's observation of the earth's orbit around the sun went against the Church's preferred interpretation of a few verses in the Hebrew Scriptures that 'the sun rises and the sun sets, and hurries back to where it rises' to mean that the sun revolved around the earth.

Earlier Christians had been more humble and cautious. Saint Augustine in the fifth century had said:

> the universe was brought into being in a less than
> fully formed state but was gifted with the capacity to
> transform itself from unformed matter into a truly
> marvellous array of structures and life forms.

This would sit easily with Darwin's discovery of the law of natural selection and mutation.

But equally the Genesis story appears to hold up. The universe had a beginning (i.e., the Big Bang) and had not, as atheists previously believed, always existed, thereby ruling out a creation and creator. Yet, science has posited, some 13.8 billion years ago, space, time and the laws of nature were born out of nothing. As Paul Davies explains in *Cosmic Jackpot*, the odds of getting a stable life- and human-friendly universe is like getting heads in a coin toss no fewer than four hundred times in a row.

True, near-impossible odds do not prove or disprove a creator, or answer why we are here. The wonderful physicist Professor Brian Cox in the BBC series *The Human Universe* seeks to give spiritual meaning or metaphysical answers to the questions 'Why are we here?', 'What is our purpose?' and 'What of the future?' As to the first question, Cox suggests that because there are an infinite number of universes we just happened to win the lottery. He concludes that there may be an infinite number of copies of you and me in an infinite number of universes and there is no particular purpose to your life and nothing special about you. To the question 'Why are we here?' he answers: You are because you had to be! What were the odds of a particular sperm finding that egg, or your parents meeting, and their parents before them, stretching back a few million years? They are all impossible odds. But no one else has done it and we did it.

One episode finishes with a Carl Sagan quote: 'For small creatures such as we the vastness is bearable only through love.' I agree with the ethical sentiment totally. But I need to assert it is also a spiritual statement and a faith leap as much as I acknowledge my own beliefs are a faith leap. After all, might not speck-like smallness and insignificance just as logically lead to 'bearing the vastness' with cruelty and selfishness? There is something else included in this calculation in order to arrive at love.

Cox says we, as possibly the only intelligent civilisation in the universe, are indescribably precious. For educated and elite scientists, protecting our rare and valuable civilisation may well serve as their main metaphysical or spiritual purpose. But I doubt that is enough to galvanise the energies of those in poverty and despair.

I do appreciate the perspective Professor Brian Cox and many humanist, nonbelieving scientists bring. I think perspective is critical and, being both fed by faith and at times fed up with the prejudices of narrow faith perspectives, I can travel a long way with Cox. To understand that the Milky Way comprises 200 to 400 billion stars and our sun is one of a trillion suns certainly shifts perspective. We do not hold a special place and are not essential. We may be indescribably precious, but that does not give us special status.

Cox concludes that we have made a glorious ascent in understanding our insignificance. We know our true place in nature, that we are such a small insignificant part of it — but what an achievement of a scientific civilisation to just know it.

As NASA launches probes for life and coded mathematic messages are transmitted millions of light years away in attempts to communicate with intelligent life, we desperately do not want to feel alone. But there is a faith perspective that says our insignificance and smallness is not the final word. As the only planet with enough water to support life, maybe the spiritual insight is that we are not alone but are loved and known by a Supreme Being. David the Psalmist says:

> When I consider your heavens, the work of your fingers, the moon and stars, what are humans that you are mindful of them? … Yet you have crowned them with glory and honour.

This is comforting. We are important in a universe that has seen existence, consciousness, wonder and love and triumph. I do not believe that existence or Being can emerge from non-existence. So faith in the primordial love that is the energy sustaining our being is significant for me.

The famous picture *Earthrise*, taken by the Apollo 8 astronauts as they glided over the surface of the moon, shows the delicate blue jewel of our planet floating in the blackness of space. 'In the beginning God created the heavens and the earth … and the spirit moved over the face of the earth …'

Australian civil religion

As Australians, we need an inspiring myth to bolster our identity. The bloodlessness of an identity cemented in the rule of law as one of the world's oldest continuing democracies does not exactly stir the national soul.

Growing up, I was proud of my grandfather because he fought at Gallipoli. I proudly told all my schoolmates he was there fighting the Turks and the Germans. I once asked him why he signed up and he said simply for God, empire and country.

Gallipoli is regarded by Australians as the birthplace of the nation because it was the first time we fought not as six independent colonies but as a nation. That first national battle at the Dardanelles peninsula on 25 April 1915 is regarded as deeply symbolic. Every ANZAC Day those who fought are honoured as the de facto fathers of the nation. It was only after my grandfather died that my uncle and my brother looked up his war records and discovered he wasn't actually at Gallipoli. He was English-born and did enlist in Australia; he did fight and he got shot and wounded in his leg, which was how he met and married my Australian-born grandmother, who nursed him. But his experience of the war was on the Western Front in France. Despite his courage being unblemished, I still felt very let down.

My mother insists that, though she also assumed he was there and told us this, her father was a scrupulously honest man who would not have deliberately misled us. The mistake, she believes now, lies in the fact that he was also a rather boring, long-winded conversationalist. He would answer her every question as a child with 'Well, yes and no, Annie' and seemed to believe that any answer that took less than hour was clearly inadequate. So my mother realises now that she hadn't really listened to him talk about the war and just made assumptions. I knew what she meant, as I had often found myself afraid to ask him a question because of such baffling encounters. But I was still disappointed about his war record.

Why was it so important to me? I think the yearning was because I wanted a personal connection to a national birth story. I expect this was my need to buy into a bit of civil religion. ANZAC Day has become Australia's most sacred day, with a dawn service in every town and tens of thousands attending in the main cities.

With the receding of religious faith, war commemoration has filled the vacuum — even though it was, in Australia's case, a total defeat and disaster. That only intensifies its deeper mystery. Now, I believe it is a good rallying point for a secular nation and, believe me, there are much more dangerous myths than ANZAC Day. But the religious overtones of our observance of it are striking.

There are shrines around the country built for the 'mighty dead'. There's an eternal flame and a liturgy written by Laurence Binyon: 'They shall not grow old, as we who are left grow old … At the going down of the sun and in the morning we will remember them.' There is haunting, sacred military music: the Last Post and the Reveille. There is a minute's silence, which is perfect for an inclusive civil religion. (It was a compromise agreed to because, historically, Catholics and Protestants could not agree on a prayer for the ANZAC service when the tradition began.) And in this honouring of those who sacrificed their lives, there is the sublime connection expressed in national bonding and community. We meditate on their deaths as 'being for us' with the words, 'Greater love has no man than this, that he lay down his life for his friends'. Words repeated in hushed solemnity. Most are totally ignorant as to the source of these words in the Gospel of John, but they are such a perfect sentiment for this sacred day, who would quibble? And then there is the holy pilgrimage to ANZAC Cove in Turkey, which increasing numbers of Australians aspire to try to do at least once in their lives. Is this not our form of the Muslim Haj, their pilgrimage to Mecca at least once in their lives?

But great religions need a creed to live by, and there is a secular creed coming out of Gallipoli. We call it mateship. Young Australians, regardless of cultural background and birthplace, are prepared in school to participate in this remembrance: Australians born in Vietnam, Turkey, Germany and Japan (all nations

Australia has fought in past wars) are all swept up into the national birth story.

This is now part of our national myth. When asked by the media what ANZAC Day means, young people are deeply moved and reply, 'They died so we might be free.' Of course, the knowing cringe. Were the Turks ever threatening us? Well, no. The Turks were actually defending their home and we were the invaders. Whose national salvation was at stake? Well, not one nation was actually threatening us in the Great War.

Yet the Turks have been more than gracious to the tens of thousands of Aussies who turn up every year, trying to experience this birth story. Kemal Atatürk's letter to the mothers in Australia to 'weep not for your sons as since they lie in our soil they are now our sons' is a beautiful sentiment that brings a tear to many eyes at ANZAC Day celebrations, but there is no hard evidence that it was Ataturk himself who wrote it. But that is the power of an identity myth. Is it possible to celebrate this event and still speak the truth? War is horrible, and videos interviewing Gallipoli veterans in the 1970s are startling. Not only did they never want to revisit the place, many saw it as a pointless sacrifice that wasted the flower of a generation and left those who survived in a living hell of trauma, depression, family violence and alcoholism. In their experience, the nation wasn't born; it was thrown into a deep malaise and massive loss of confidence that continued right through the next twenty years and the Great Depression.

It is possible to honour the sacrifice and still say our leaders failed. Failed militarily as, even if we had won at Gallipoli and not suffered an appalling defeat, it would not have changed anything in the Great War. Failed politically, as Churchill had to resign as first Lord of the Admiralty for his disastrous Gallipoli plan and went in disgrace to fight on the Western Front. And failed personally, as Rudyard Kipling, the great booster of British imperialism, experienced. In 1915 his son John enlisted. Within weeks John died on the Western Front at the age of eighteen. In bitterness, Kipling wrote, 'If any question why we died/Tell them, because our fathers lied'. Many believe Kipling's personal trust in imperialism and the genius of British leaders was utterly shattered.

Secularism and the public square

Recently I was the subject of some confusion between radio presenters in my home city of Melbourne. Red Symons asked Jon Faine, the presenter of the morning show, 'So who is coming up on your program?'

Jon replied, 'Well, in the "Conversation Hour" my co-host is the Baptist preacher Tim Costello.'

Red Symons reacted with surprise. 'Why do you call him a preacher? I really like Tim, but I see him as a social justice campaigner, not a preacher!'

Jon replied, 'Well, yes, he is an advocate for the poor but as a reverend he is primarily a Baptist preacher. What's your problem with that?'

Red shot back, 'I am just very uncomfortable calling him that.' Red Symons clearly thought 'preacher' a negative, even a pejorative, label. I suspect Jon, as an atheist, does too, and was enjoying needling Red. I appreciate that in another sense Red was defending me and saying that, in his mind, I don't fit that negative stereotype of a censorious finger-wagger.

All this is to illustrate the growing sway of secularity in our society. It was if they were saying, 'I like his values, but please spare me his beliefs.' But values do not materialise out of thin air. When they are connected to faith, and an expression of it, why are we so allergic? I completely support the notion of secularity when it means no one group is privileged in the public square. This understanding of the word 'secular' is essential. I am a very strong supporter of secular government and a secular public square but not a secularism that suppresses those beliefs.

Baptists were the ones who fought for separation of church and state because they were dissenters wanting to worship as their conscience dictated. In Baptist Thomas Helwys's *Mystery of Iniquity* he powerfully argued that the king was his sovereign in political power, but not the sovereign over his soul or a Buddhist or atheist soul. The state has authority but it does not have ultimacy; that belonged to God. Stated another way: the state is not to be worshipped!

How can compromise coexist with absolutes? Herein lies the genius of church–state separation. In societies where there is Islamic scriptural literalism, Sharia law is the civil and criminal code of the whole nation. How can it be compromised on its prescription for amputating thieves' hands or killing adulterers if it is the Messenger Mohammed declaring the truth of Allah? Compromise is an insult to Allah's revealed word in the Qur'an. In Christian societies adultery was once criminalised, until we decided it was a moral failure against God and one's partner — not an infraction against the state.

A secular state saves us from tyranny and all 'ism's — even secularism itself. It saves us from communism and atheism and Hinduism, Islamism or Christianism. Without it a ferocious religious certainty imposes its truth and refuses dissent, threatening minorities. When religion is believed to be the absolute truth then any compromise is a sin and becomes impossible. It is secular government alone that can allow us to live together in tolerance, avoiding the conflict that is inevitable between clashing absolutist theocracies. Politics is the art of compromise so we can all at least coexist. In a democracy conflict is resolved by a majority: a majority vote wins. So whatever the absolutist claims of a minority, their choice is civil disobedience but still accepting the secular majority vote enshrined in law. I am extraordinarily relieved that we have a secular ideal for the most powerful entity that humans have invented for justice and order: the secular state. But I only support a secular approach if it means every view is welcome and has an equal standing in the public square.

Faith and the secular

I live the tension between faith and the secular. Secular people generally welcome what I say but suggest I drop the spiritual mush; religious people are disappointed that I have not turned up the volume on faith. The chasm between the two camps seems to be growing. Maybe I am foolish to try to span it.

Clearly, people are fed up with faith. Certainly religious faith is seen to be questionable, even harmful, in the West. Islam may be the main source of the fear, but Christianity is also deeply on the nose; even violent racist Buddhist monks in Burma and Sri Lanka have besmirched the reputation of their religion.

I know people are sick of Christians reminding them that Western civilisation emerged to some degree from the Judaeo-Christian story. Usually it is the arrogance that follows that is irritating; the presumption of a privileged stance from which to lecture, impose and even to veto change. A secular society says all views are welcome in public debate and the shaping of public policy, and no view is automatically given a special authority. I totally agree. Can we not tolerantly disagree with each other while still respecting the right to religious freedom, and all still accept a majority vote after debate regardless of whether our side won or lost?

Secular society is not without its flaws. Many wonder where values come from without a spirituality. Even militant secularists sometimes worry about the vacuum in moral vision left with the demise of the Church. Where do we look now for morality and guidance? Politicians? The disorientation arises because we long for some 'truth', both public and private, but all is now relative, slippery and contested.

I understand 'secular' to simply mean that no view, religious or secular, no faith or claim to dogmatic truth, is privileged with the automatic backing of state power. 'Secularism', on the other hand, is a fundamentalist conviction that religion and spirituality have no place or redeeming value. This view kicks God upstairs into the realm of private belief, with no relevance for life downstairs in politics and policy.

Secularism offers more certainty in reason and scientific progress as the best path for guidance. But does it overreach with its claim to be objective? Might it not also have a blind spot by assuming that reason and secularism is never dogmatic? This approach seems to sever organic connection and allow little room for mystery. I think the explosive counter-secular growth of New Age spirituality, though eclectic, ill-defined and vague, is a strong reaction against secularism. It is an expression of longing for integration and unity. People seem clearly fed up with the faiths on offer — both religious and secular.

In trying to build a bridge between the warring camps I provocatively describe myself as a spiritual or Christian secularist. I embrace reason but do not trust it to answer meaning. I embrace faith but want it disciplined by reason. So I believe faith and secularism both have a truth; but each needs to listen to the other perspective.

A repressive secularism does not speak to our spiritual energies. I admit religion can be a negative force in the geopolitics of terror and clash of civilisations, but I believe it is much more a positive force than the public secularism that requires obedience to the law and trust in the market but leaves private morality to personal preference. This hollows out meaning and creates a loss of cohesion around a worthy public morality and common vision. That is not to suggest I want to impose one public religious morality on all, but neither is it to vacate the field and leave public morality to the whims of 'do what you like as long as you do not hurt anyone'. That approach is empty and allows an amoral market to exploit or seduce us from being the best we can be. Prestige has drifted away from theologians, poets and philosophers to neuroscientists, economists and evolutionary biologists who have little to offer in answering the ultimate questions. We argue in the public square over fiscal and tax policy, but not about how to find a vocation or measure the worth of your life. Our moral conversation happens under the pretence that we are talking about politics, which is why tax policy arguments come to resemble holy wars.

Because there are fewer places in public to talk about the things that matter most, the search for meaning loses a vocabulary and people are stripped of the ability to ask the right questions, let alone look for the right answers. We certainly do not use a spiritual vocabulary, let alone faith in God, for any big conversations. We only allow neutral categories. Productivity and efficiency are sufficient for any economic debate and utilitarianism or the happiness of the majority is sufficient for political or democratic questions. The selfish gene and genetic determinism dominates questions of behaviour and whether we can even hold people accountable for their actions. But this shrinks us.

I believe everyone is born with a moral imagination and that there is a shared belief that life is to be lived in service to some good. Religion has been an attempt to address questions about what that good is and should not be shut down by a rigid secularism that pretends to be neutral, even disinterested. To say 'leave your values and beliefs out of this — speak them only in the private domain' is to silence the most needed voices.

I am even worried about how market forces have penetrated the Church. When we start to hear a prosperity gospel preached on Sundays, I hear a message that to be poor is sinful and to be saved means we are blessed and rich. Yet the most faithful Christians that I have met around the world are poor and probably will be all their lives. But being poor materially is not the same as being poor in love, spirit, community and celebration of relationships.

Justice, human dignity and life-giving community do not arise from a market mentality. Markets have no morals. Actually, nothing is less self-evident in a global market than that all people are born equal and equally worthy of dignity. The perfectly transparent market may be more meritocratic than other interventions, but markets can supply little meaning. Nearly 1 billion people go to bed hungry every night but we dare not interfere with the power of demand and supply. The market model is now so ingrained in our society that it is used to determine policies for the common good. Productivity and efficiency are useful market concepts but cannot replace a sense of the sacred connection of all human life. But this leads to transactional relationships colonising all aspects of life, including family, friendship, community and even religion. Everything becomes a self-interested cost–benefit calculation. This hollows out true community and destroys solidarity expressed in a common good, deep relational dignity and a common hope.

The 'spiritual but not religious' are probably the fastest-growing tribe, but there are few places to organise around that. They may develop with this movement maturing, but it is hard to imagine how you build communities of resistance that can shape politics and power agendas from an individualistic spirituality. It takes institutions built on spirituality to do that, and we call them religion. Religion is the serious attempt throughout human history to give answers to permanently recurring human questions (Who am I? What is the purpose of my life? How do I tell right from wrong?) and then to organise. The questions are shared by all — spiritual, religious and unbelievers — but what we do with the answers needs focus and organisation. I think that individualism even in spirituality has failed us as so many of us feel utterly alone. Faith is personal but never individualistic. Likewise consumerism has failed to make us happy, only restless and envious of others. A triumphalism that aims at success as the goal of living has made us ashamed and fearful of failure. We need community and organised faith to address these illusions and to resist these powerful seductions.

Robert Putnam in his book *Bowling Alone* spoke of 'social capital'. It essentially means 'trust' and is as fundamental to markets working as self-interest and free exchange. The concept of social capital showed that community and relationships were essential for prosperity. Without community and the ties that bind, the economic machine cannot function. But equally, voluntary associations, such as those in sporting and recreational clubs, churches and political parties, nourish life and assist human flourishing. It is why I prefer to call not-for-profit organisations 'for purpose' organisations. There is nothing seamy and sordid about market profit, so why define ourselves negatively? Rather, we recognise a higher purpose than even profit. It is that transformative purpose which should define these organisations that inspire volunteering, love and generosity.

Now there is interest in spiritual capital. What is a transcendent connection, and what effect does that have? What are the real foundations of our trust, and how does its absence or depletion gum up our work and the whole society?

We all live in a global village, with trust in people, government and institutions receding for many young people. I see an increasing trust in the self, the market and nation or tribe. But are they worthy of this trust? The promise that each of us can experience individual identity and self-realisation through our own reason seems hollow.

Reason and secularism are not worthy of uncritical trust, either; they have themselves been subverted to serve capitalism, communism and fascism. Half of all German physicians joined the Nazi's Physicians League and ran the sterilisation and euthanasia programs. Judges implemented the Nuremberg laws and academics dismissed Jewish colleagues and banned books without protest. Reason certainly serves capitalism and nationalism. The American Psychologists Association has acknowledged that they breached their own professional standards by supplying psychologists to certify that torture and waterboarding were acceptable. Even free and democratic societies can twist reason to serve evil ends. We listen to politicians lecture us about the great entrepreneurs in our nation and their service and philanthropy while they demonise welfare cheats and the poor. But the trust that we are all pulling our weight and paying our tax has been totally shattered.

As Dick Gross said, in defending Christianity at a Melbourne Town Hall panel while I was being subjected to the usual grilling about Christianity's evils, secular people should avoid a body count because the calculus is not very flattering to atheists. Indeed, Stalin, Mao and Pol Pot — all reputedly on the atheist team — were responsible for the killing of millions. And Dick, as an atheist, offered publicly that he is never blamed for this while I regularly get blamed for religious violence.

Self-esteem is not enough

The self-esteem culture aims at success and churns out a lot of aphorisms about ourselves as own saviour; e.g., 'The best place to find a helping hand is at the end of your arm.' While self-love can be liberating and exhilarating, we can never find lasting meaning and resilience in life's trouble if we think we are the centre. Whether we believe in God or something else, we need transcendence beyond ourselves. Expecting and attempting great things only for ourselves is a recipe for despair and soul sickness. The beginning of true faith and robust spirituality is the realisation that it is not all about me.

Neither is attempting great things a straightforward path. I want young people to spot the nonsense in the popular belief that 'you can be whatever you want to be'. Few of us can be Nelson Mandela or Mother Teresa, although we can choose to share in their wider vision.

We need to sniff critically at the self-realisation gospel preached by most of the gurus. I get furious at the shallow message of positive psychology thoughtlessly pumped into young people. I know at school-presentation nights (and I speak at a lot of them) it's basically the same kids who win the prizes every year.

What messages are we giving to the rest — keep trying and you might receive the encouragement prize? Yet I know there are kids not being applauded on the stage who have in truth travelled a greater distance in effort and improvement than those pulling off the award.

Instead of trying to be whoever you want to be, attempt to be what God made you to be and it will be better for you and the world. Stop comparing up, as there is always someone who seems to be doing better. Compare down and you will immediately realise how blessed you already are. Question what success really means and you will discover it is in being true to your own potential and knowing your inner purpose, which is much more solid ground. Competition has its downsides and feting the winners narrows the exquisite joy in just participating. What is wrong with being ordinary? Much better to be ordinary, even struggling, but fulfilled.

Teachers of Gen Y kids tell me how the 'you can be whatever you want to be' mentality is smashing these kids' resilience. It infects their attitude to everything they try. Failure is shameful. How do they know what's worth doing without a wider purpose? With parents who have sacrificed so much requiring them to succeed, this generation is under pressure. They must succeed or their self-identity is at risk. But this can be paralysing.

I hear these teachers tell me that study is no longer a soul-inspiring search for a life worth living rooted in the great traditions of philosophy, religion and culture's transcendent stories. Instead, students are anxious and demand specifics from their lecturers. They simply want the best grade; the outcome, not the process, is everything. But wisdom teaches us that we learn much more in the process than in even well-graded outcomes. We learn much more from our failures (if we respond to the lesson) than we do from our successes.

When I started at university if you were really smart you might do philosophy and literature in an arts degree; if you were a plodder you did commerce or a business degree. We felt sorry for those students, as it was only glorified counting! Now look at the prized degrees; it's certainly not an arts degree. Now, if you are really smart you have an MBA in business.

The self-aware brain

We non-scientists now know, thanks to the author of *The Brain That Changes Itself*, that our brains are more plastic than hardware and can rewire themselves with touch, sound, exercise and meditation or prayer. Formerly we thought that, once damaged, a brain could no more fix itself than an electronics circuit board could after it fused. But that is wrong. Now we know that the right stimuli, when combined particularly with exercise, can result in self-repair. So there is a lot of discussion about how the constant interruptions of Twitter, gaming and email are rewiring the brains of young people, who have only known this interactive world. Many believe technology is changing attention spans and reducing our capacity to engage in serious contemplation. And all this change is happening in a context where we are more sedentary, which is fatal for changes to the brain.

There is no doubt that new communities and friendships are being formed online; it is not all downside. But how are our brains rewiring? Does a life increasingly lived online increase soul sickness and threaten the pursuit of a deeper meaning? Does it neutralise emotional solidarity and our capacity to read the emotional nuances of others?

I was in a Chinese restaurant in Melbourne for lunch and saw a group of ten friends in their early twenties eating their meal in silence. Not a word was uttered for twenty minutes because they were all focused on their phones. I was so struck with this silent socialising that I went up a bit closer and took a picture. They didn't even notice or look up!

I wonder at the rewiring of my own brain. I come from a family where lunch could be a two-hour affair, yet I have become shockingly impatient. The other day I rushed into a Hungry Jack's and ordered a burger and fries. I was in a hurry, but the woman behind the counter politely told me there would be a five-minute wait for the burger. To my shame, I felt rage rise up inside me. I heard myself asking sharply, 'But excuse me: Why the delay?'

The woman looked a bit surprised, but professionally looked me straight in the eye and said, 'Because we are cooking the food.' I am even more shocked to admit that I nearly blurted out, 'What are you cooking the food for? I'm in a hurry!' Thankfully I checked myself, but I was still irritated. I had to do some self-talk and remind myself that, even at a fast food venue, they probably still have to cook the food. I should know better, but such is the speed of life we get impatient at the merest inconvenience.

Faith is the new black

I have been informed recently that my old alma mater, Monash University, is treating religion and spirituality with more academic respect than they did when I was studying law there. Monash University Medical School now gets its students to take a course in Spirituality as Health Enhancement. It covers religion, spirituality and meaning. The course teaches that spirituality has a profound impact upon mental and physical health. It aims to teach 'science engendering wonder'. It focuses on how spiritual or religious views affect ethical issues such as euthanasia, suicide, abortion, contraception and blood transfusion.

The course exists because research has shown that 83 per cent of patients wanted doctors to ask about their spiritual beliefs; it was no longer just medical advice they were after, but a meaningful exchange encouraging their doctor's understanding of their needs and hopes. This is particularly important when a patient's illness is terminal or requires life-saving measures.

This course teaches that sometimes religious belief can clash with medical care and can have major implications, but that the empirical data shows that religious commitment is beneficial in preventing mental and physical illness and in facilitating recovery. It is protective for both depression and suicide, and also for physical illness. Belief improves longevity and mortality rates.

Now, some may say this is just a placebo effect. But the fact that so many improve when taking placebos because they believe they have been treated with the real drug proves the point: belief and meaning matter in treatment.

In any event we now know it is more than a placebo. Many studies have found that the faith–happiness correlation is overwhelming. They correlated religious attendance with life satisfaction, engagement in community and well-being among the elderly and showed twice as much reported happiness in the religious. These studies extended comparisons of the irreligious with religious to coping with crises and loss. The religious had dramatically lower rates of depression and psychiatric disorders, delinquency, abuse of drugs and suicide levels. This is not a proof of the existence of God — but maybe it shows how faith creates communities and trust, which translates into great social supports. Faith counteracts the rampant individualism that many believe is responsible for elevated rates of depression. It builds community and reciprocal rights and responsibilities.

But not everyone is comfortable in a religious community.

Some years ago I was on the coastline of northern New South Wales speaking at a New Age festival with hundreds of young people attending. Although their crystal beads, soft drugs, skinny-dipping and aura readings were not exactly my cup of tea I loved the seriousness they showed in seeking spiritual answers and an alternative to the materialism of our culture. They had an earnestness that touched me. I remember mentioning in my session that I knew a number of young people like them, with the same heart hungers and asking the same spiritual questions, in churches around the nation. The festival-goers seemed genuinely shocked that anyone would think of pursuing such important questions in a church. Many were not in the least bit antagonistic: it was just a totally novel thought that the Church would even be interested in spirituality.

How far has the Church come in blowing it? These young seekers were very attracted to Jesus and what he taught. They loved the product but almost universally had contempt for the retail outlet. Now I get that the reputation of the Church has been almost totally trashed in our nation by its shameful complicity in child abuse. Without excusing what should be higher standards in the Church, the same breach of trust has been exhibited in the military, schools, scouts and even our much-loved secular Children's Hospital. The root of these abuses is misguided tribal loyalty that protects identity at all costs, not religious belief itself.

But the Church will bounce back. At the Sunday Easter service in 1742 at St Paul's Cathedral in London there were only eight people in attendance in that huge church. Christianity was on the nose and was thought to be dying. Then an Anglican minister called John Wesley did the unthinkable. He started preaching the Gospel to the poor outside the church, in fields and pubs and open markets. The rigid Anglican hierarchy intent on protecting the brand were shocked and bishops refused to give him a licence to preach in their own dioceses. Everyone in the Church hierarchy believed that the Gospel could only be preached from pulpits in sanctified places like churches. John Wesley ignored the need to get a licence from a bishop when he entered his diocese and provocatively said 'the whole world is my parish'.

Paraphrased, he was giving the middle finger to the institution and suggesting that the world, even in profane places, is alive with God. A massive Christian revival occurred among the uneducated, resulting in the closing of gin palaces and ameliorating crime and domestic violence. This meant not only filling the churches again, but also influencing the nation not to follow the madness of the French Revolution. On his deathbed John Wesley's last letter was to a young politician named William Wilberforce, asking him to fight the 'execrable slave trade' with all his might. In the developing world among the poor the churches, temples and mosques are still packed. If the Church can relinquish its proprietary licences, young people will always be attracted to hope and good news.

The spiritual search is still alive in Australia. In this most secular nation there are far more Australians in church each Sunday than all the crowds attending professional football and other sports each week. That will come as a surprise to many, as we all know what a sports-obsessed nation we are. Also it will come as a surprise that twenty-three of the twenty-five biggest charities in Australia are Christian faith–based. In the US, a much more obviously church-attending society, it is only ten out of twenty-five, and in the UK it's three out of twenty-five. The Church's organisations continue to do much of the heavy charitable lifting in a proudly secular nation.

Pope Francis may do much to help heal the Church's reputation. It's very interesting to me that many of my atheist and secular friends will quote and praise this pope, where before his advent they were utterly hostile to Catholicism. It tells me that when a Church leader focuses on the product, not the outlet, there is almost a yearning to believe and re-engage.

This pope, when asked about the Church's attitudes to homosexuality and gay people, said, 'What do I know and who am I to judge?' This response is precisely aligned with Jesus' warning to his followers to 'Judge not lest you be judged' and his demand that they not cast the first stone. Here is a pope who speaks out about the distressing inequality that capitalism creates, and who publicly criticises the greed and gossip in the Vatican. He refuses to sleep in a Vatican palace but lives in a humble room; he serves Rome's homeless and washed the feet of a Muslim woman, a Brazilian transsexual person and inmates at a juvenile detention centre. At Easter Thursday mass in St Peter's Basilica in 2016 it was the first time that women could have their feet washed by priests; previously that privilege was only available to men.

He has made many unpopular political stances: he was the first pope to recognise that Armenians suffered the genocide of 1 million–plus people in 1915 at the hands of Ottoman Turks, much to the outrage of the Turks. His recognition of the Palestinian State infuriates the Israeli prime minister. His meeting with lifelong Cuban communist Raúl Castro was so life-changing it prompted Castro to say he was thinking of becoming a Catholic. Finally, he has acknowledged that climate change is real and that we need to draw on spiritual resources to stop polluting our garden and putting the poor of the earth at the greatest risk. True, he has not changed many of the Catholic sticking points or surrendered his position — but he has changed the tone. It sounds like grace and good news, not superiority, self-righteousness and judgement.

A 2010 Barna Group study in the US asked respondents to spontaneously identify words when they heard the name 'Jesus'. Out poured words like courage, love, tolerance, self-sacrifice, justice and divinity. When asked to do the same with the word 'church', responses like intolerance, hypocrisy, judgement, child abuse, self-righteousness, wealth and legalism topped the list. Could the unpopularity of the Church be due to people's reasonable expectation that the Church should be more like Jesus? Where on earth did they stumble onto such a novel idea? Maybe the retail outlet's unpopularity is due to its utter failure in matching the integrity of its product.

Let me add that there are many churches that are thriving with relevant worship and extraordinary programs for the young. To the cynics watching megachurches such as Hillsong attracting the young, I would ask: Don't you prefer these young people to be serving and giving and inspired in church rather than clubbing all night and taking party drugs? As they worship with hands raised I know that so many are seeking to live out their faith in service and make a difference.

A few years ago my wife and I attended the hilarious Broadway hit *The Book of Mormon*. The plot goes like this: two Mormon missionaries sent out from Salt Lake City to Uganda find themselves in a community riddled with HIV/AIDS, polluted water, gender oppression and a militia leader raping the women and enslaving them. The missionaries are total novices who lose the plot and screw up the Mormon message so badly that, when the Mormon elders visit, the missionaries are excommunicated. The elders are shocked at the syncretism of the recently converted African Mormons and kick them out of the Church, destroying their hopes of moving to Salt Lake City, their promised land. The converts are shattered by this rejection. But through their grief the Ugandans realise that, despite their rejection by the official Mormon Church, their home has changed and they no longer need to emigrate to Salt Lake City. The spread of HIV/AIDS has stopped, they have clean water, the girls are in school and the militia leader is now a peaceful Mormon family man (keeping his wives). Here is the power of transcendent belief. Even if it is a bastardised Mormon placebo, it worked. There are not too many cynical musicals lampooning religion that you leave inspired by hope, yet that's exactly what my wife and I experienced.

Religion has also played a role in the World Bank's audacious goal to eliminate absolute poverty by the year 2030. Dr Jim Yong Kim knew that technocratic plans, however smart, cannot deliver development outcomes without alignment with religious faiths. Holy men and religious institutions are still the main cultural force and spiritual glue in many societies, and people will only be committed to change if they see these development goals framed in the language of their faith. The result is a remarkable document written about the moral and spiritual imperative called 'Our Common Understanding'. It sets out a shared moral consensus between all the great faiths to respond to the many in the world living in degrading conditions. The religious leaders pledge to lead a compelling vision to end extreme poverty by the year 2030.

Faith is clearly experiencing a resurgence, from courses offered in medical schools to the World Bank to the arts. I know that if I had a church with all the Christians in Australia who still believe but no longer attend church, it would be the biggest megachurch in Australia by a country mile. But just because they no longer attend church does not mean that all these disparate people and groups are not committed to pursuing spiritual meaning.

Spiritual meaning is how people find solace in times of tragedy. I cannot explain why people suffer from natural disasters or innocent children endure terrible disabilities. I have read the various explanations of where evil comes from, and I worry that too many of these answers seek to exonerate God, from 'people do not have enough faith' to 'God has a deeper plan and purpose'. I believe that God, in creating us, made us in his image but he did not merely duplicate himself. So I understand that humans have a different, independent existence; we are not just replicas of God. When that freedom results in selfishness, racism, sexism and militarism, God cannot be blamed for the choices we make. But while I can get my head around war, violence and greed, which are human-made suffering, natural catastrophes and the suffering of the innocent are another issue. I do not know where that comes from. I cannot intellectually reconcile the suffering caused by such disasters with the good, creative and loving God I believe in. But, although understanding is important for meaning and meaning matters most to me, I have no answer to the puzzle. Even without comprehensive answers I find I still believe. Call it foolishness or dishonesty, but I know that without this trust I would find myself less equipped to respond to the human suffering, whether caused by war and famine or cyclones, earthquakes and tsunamis, that has occupied my professional life at World Vision.

Spiritual knowing is not the same as scientific knowledge. Spirituality takes mystery seriously. Even atheists like John Dewey wanted religion taught in schools because he recognised this form of knowing. We know the religious impulse is deeply rooted in human nature: from at least 50,000 years ago there is evidence of rituals and symbols we used to give us meaning.

With the advent of the alphabet about 5000 BCE, profound questions about meaning and purpose could be shared. The ancient Greeks called it philosophy, but it was still religious discourse. Of course, the advent of the printing press in the 1530s spread the Bible and spurred the Protestant Reformation, but it also gave rise to science. Different ideas could be spread and tested and analysed.

The Reformation God was separate from his creation, so you could experiment on nature without blasphemously experimenting on God. This aided science but, by objectifying nature, it snapped a religious link with nature's mystery and rendered many rituals questionable, like the Hopi Indians' rising before dawn each day to pray the sun up. This story may be apocryphal but, as I heard it, when an anthropologist suggested they try an experiment and sleep in for just one morning they refused. When asked why, they said, 'And what — plunge the whole world into total darkness for the sake of your stupid experiment?' And at a deeper-meaning level they were right. The meaning and rhythm of their lives, culture and community would have been shattered. We are still struggling with this loss of purpose.

The Protestant Reformation in a sense ushered in the first scientific religion, with assertions about the inerrant word of God and scriptural truth in geology and history and science. Inevitably it led to critical methods being applied to the Bible as much as to non-sacred literature to test authorship and influences, which undermined its authority.

I still believe the religious knowing in the stories in the Bible. I believe that creation is good, not bad. That it was not born in violence, as some religious traditions have it. It is a gift. Beauty and awe nourish me and this permits me to live with joy and vitality. I do not resent or fear Galileo's discovery that the sun did not revolve around the earth, highlighting our smallness and the insignificance of our planet. The religious fear of this discovery was, simply: If we are not central then how are we the apex of God's creation?

I actually like the mystery that our minor, off-Broadway galaxy alone contains over 100 billion stars, many with their attendant planets. Add to that maybe 100 billion other observable galaxies and boy are we small and insignificant. But it is still the planet that I happen to love, live on and need to find meaning in. I am comfortable with the unfolding scientific insights into the universe's beginning. But I still confess faith in a source of being or Creator. I am happy to leave to the scientists the 'how' of the beginning. The creation story is important to answer the 'why'.

Faith is important in science. It took many years to empirically prove Einstein's mathematically elegant theory of relativity. But many of our theories today are beyond our power of observation and proof, with many scientists saying we have to accept that empirical verification — the scientific method — must be abandoned. We have to just trust the theoretical formula. After all, how do you test multiple universes or string theory? But we are already allowing these theories to underpin our thinking without assuming proof. In the same way, we can allow faith to undergird us without demanding proof of God's existence. After all, there is still mystery in this world.

Conclusion

Spirituality is deeply personal, but I do not think it should ever be individualistic. To do so breaks the connection and interdependence with others, with the mystery of life and the transcendent. It's why I love each Tuesday morning when our World Vision staff have the opportunity to come together to reflect, meditate and pray for our world. It is both a moving personal time and an inspiring communal event. We start with an Indigenous acknowledgement of country, then we read, listen to a message and sometimes sing. But we always finish with the same prayer. We recite this aloud and leave feeling refocused. This prayer sums up my spirituality. It is how my faith engages the small and the big challenges.

Liturgy:

SOLO VOICE:
May God bless us with discomfort …

ALL:
Discomfort at easy answers,
half truths,
and superficial relationships;
so that we may live from deep
within our hearts.

SOLO VOICE:
May God bless us with
anger …

ALL:
Anger at injustice,
oppression, and
exploitation of people and our earth;
so that we may work for justice, freedom and peace.

SOLO VOICE:
May God bless us with
tears to shed …

ALL:
Tears for those who suffer from pain,
rejection, starvation and war;
so that we may reach out our hand
to comfort them
and turn their pain into joy.

SOLO VOICE:
And may God bless us with
foolishness …

ALL:
Enough foolishness to believe that we can make a difference
    in this world;
so that we can do
what others claim cannot be done.
Amen.